T5-CQA-879

REAL HUNTING

WITH NAHC MEMBERS

NORTH AMERICAN HUNTING CLUB

MINNETONKA, MINNESOTA

REAL HUNTING

WITH NAHC MEMBERS

Tom Carpenter
Creative Director

Heather Koshiol
Book Development Coordinator

Greg Schwieters
Book Design and Production

Laura Holle
Book Development Assistant

Patrick Durkin
Editorial Production

4 5 6 7 8 / 08 07 06 05
ISBN 1-58159-172-1
© 2002 North American Hunting Club

North American Hunting Club
12301 Whitewater Drive
Minnetonka, MN 55343
www.huntingclub.com

All photos from NAHC members except:
Charles Alsheimer 1 (top right & left), 10, 40, 43, 50, 72, 84; **Lance Beeny** 138; **Don Jones** 1 (bottom left), 6, 8, 16, 20, 21, 30, 32, 44, 70, 76, 90, 96, 150, 152; **Mark Kayser** cover, 1 (bottom right), 124, 131, 148; **Lee Kline** 17, 80, 82, 88, 98, 104, 110, 114, 136; **Bob Robb** 99; **Jim Van Norman**, 5; **Ben Williams** 126; **NAHC/Jeff Boehler** 53 (top); **NAHC/Tom Carpenter** 67; **NAHC/Gordy Krahn** 139, 140, 142 (both), 143, 144, 145 (both), 146; **NAHC/Greg Schwieters** 34, 36, 45, 154; **NAHC/Jim Van Norman** 33 (both), 41, 42, 48, 49, 51, 53 (bottom), 54, 55, 56, 57, 59, 60, 61, 65, 66, 58 (both), 62 (both), 78, 86 (both), 95, 97, 102 (both), 103 (all), 106, 107, 108, 109 (both), 118 (both), 119, 120, 121, 122 (all), 123 (both), 129, 131, 134 (both), 135, 153 (both), 156, 157.

Illustrations: David Sidley 133; **NAHC/Dave Schelitzche** 14, 64, 69, 77, 97, 105, 128.

REAL HUNTING

TABLE OF CONTENTS

Chapter 1 — Family & Friends 8

Chapter 2 — Deer 34

Chapter 3 — Turkey 70

Chapter 4 — Big Game 88

Chapter 5 — Adventure 110

Chapter 6 — Game Birds 124

Chapter 7 — Predators 136

Chapter 8 — Small Game 148

WELCOME TO REAL HUNTING

It's fun to read about adventures to faraway hinterlands, and imagine yourself on the excursion. In fact, many North American Hunting Club members travel—sooner or later, often or not—to special places to pursue new game.

But if you're like most of us, you traditionally do much of your hunting a little closer to home—for the game we all love, such as whitetails, turkeys, upland birds, predators, small game, even some big game beyond deer. These are the topics that occupy the bulk of our hunting thoughts and time.

So here is *Real Hunting*: a picture-filled collection of stories and strategies, tales and tips, legends and lore, direct to you from fellow NAHC members. These pages will entertain you, make you laugh, make you remember, make you think, make you feel something a little down deep … and make you a better hunter too.

And as you read the pages that follow, you will learn something else: How very much hunting means to your fellow NAHC Members, how knowledgeable they are about their passion, and how generous they are in sharing with you what they feel and what they know.

Everything here reflects your kind of hunting: Real stories you can relate to. Real ideas that work. All from real people who hunt just as hard as you and I. There's no better author than NAHC members!

Fantasies are fine, special trips are fun. But it's *Real Hunting* that fills our souls and keeps us out there hunting hard and doing what we love best.

Tom Carpenter
Editor—North American Hunting Club Books

FAMILY & FRIENDS

We hunt for many reasons beyond killing game.

Of course, wild places draw us with their beauty, quiet and solitude ... and let us escape everyday life.

But hunting also helps us find something else: relationships. Hunting creates special bonds that bring friends together, family closer.

MIRACLE IN MIDDLEBURGH

For as long as I can remember, I watched my father come home with a buck every hunting season. He taught our family, including my mother, how to hunt. I always asked Dad why he never mounted any of the 6- and 8-pointers he shot, and he always said the same thing: "For me to mount a deer, it has to be at least an 8-pointer, and it must have a big rack with nice, thick antlers. It definitely has to have a perfect match from side to side."

I couldn't believe that after 50 years of dropping bucks not one met those standards for the wall, but my father sure had fun taking us four kids deer hunting. It was our closest bond.

Our family endured a terrible setback when my brother Angelo died in an accident at age 23. At that time, Dad's favorite hunting spots were just about finished in the Hancock, New York, area, and Sal and I were old enough to hunt big game. It took me eight years to get my first deer, a doe. Sal got a big 6-pointer out of Hancock before we stopped hunting there.

We then started hunting in Middleburgh, New York, where my parents bought 42 acres of land. It was frustrating sometimes not seeing a buck on our property, but I did come across a big spike and shot him. My dad always told us just to enjoy our hunt and the beautiful woods; getting a deer was a bonus.

The miracle involved a perfect 8-pointer ... and one very special twist.

At one point a few years ago, I had missed two seasons because I had been living in Virginia and then California. But I was happy to hear Dad on the phone when he told me about a 5-pointer he got. That joy turned to shock and grief when I later got a call informing me that Dad had been hit by a van and killed. He had been on his way home to Long Island on the last day of deer season. I still can't believe it. I remind myself to be glad he got to hunt until the day he died.

I flew home on a plane to go to the wake and funeral, knowing I'd be back to stay near Mom. I was in another world during all the funeral services. But just before they closed the casket, knowing I would never see him again, something made me say, "Dad, next year on opening day I'll drop that big 8-pointer with the kind of rack you would have put on the wall."

I had a year to think about that promise. I never went a day without praying for that deer. I often wondered what I had gotten myself into. How could I promise such a perfect rack on a big 8-pointer when I had never even seen one like it before? In almost 50 years of hunting, my father never got one like that. But every day I would kiss the picture that showed him with an 8-pointer, and say: "Please God, please Dad, send me this deer and I'll drop him with one shot, and that will let me know you're able to see me. And when I walk this mountain, you're walking it with me."

Opening day finally arrived. It was so sad to walk up that hill with Dad's gun, knowing I wouldn't see him come out of his spot, and knowing I wouldn't hear his whistle. I was actually crying as I walked up the hill. Things got a little back to normal when I shot a big doe later in the morning. I had a hard time dragging it out of the woods in a foot of snow. I had been through back surgery a few years before, and I've had problems ever since.

After lunch, I was in so much pain I couldn't walk forward. I had to walk sideways, and my brother and cousin had to pick up my legs for me to get into the truck. As I started back up the hill with Dad's gun, I was again crying, saying I couldn't even make it up there. Why had I put all this pressure on myself by promising I would get the kind of deer I had never seen in 18 years of hunting?

Just as I finished that thought, I heard an ATV coming my way. It was a guy I had met earlier that day. He said, "It looks like you could use a ride." Man, it was like an angel had come to my rescue. In no time I was at the top of the mountain. I had been sitting no longer than five minutes when I saw a deer heading my way. For some reason, I knew it was a buck, and sure enough, it was. I was amazed I was so calm. I remembered what my father had always told me: "If you get lucky enough to see a buck, don't look at the horns. Just worry about where you're going to hit him."

The deer was going from my right to left. I had Dad's gun up, and for some reason, these words came out of my mouth: "Okay, Dad, as soon as he passes that tree, we'll drop him." I couldn't believe how calm I was. I felt as if I had 50 years' experience in shooting bucks, and that this was just another buck. After I shot and the deer went down, I got up and was all excited. I was saying: "Wow, I just shot my first buck. I don't know what it is, Dad, but I know you're proud of me."

As I got closer to the deer, I saw it had a big rack with thick antlers. When I got up to it, I counted three tines on one side and both brow tines in the middle. I grabbed the rack and said, "Come

SOME WHITETAIL TIPS

Here are a few tips that helped me get this deer: First, stay confident that a buck will come up the hill at any time. Second, Dad always said: "You have to put in the time. The more you hunt, the better your chances." Third, if you see a big buck, don't stare at the antlers. Concentrate on where you can get off a good shot, and focus on the deer's chest right behind the elbow. If that shot isn't possible, shoot him in the neck. Fourth, always use a scent cover. I often place a buck lure in a 20-yard circle around my post. I also like to rub the lure on saplings along the trail to my post.

Joe Caruso
Middleburgh, New York

on, Dad, please tell me we did it." The rest of the rack was buried in the snow. I couldn't believe my eyes when I pulled it up. There it was, just like in my prayers and dreams: the perfect rack of an 8-pointer. I looked up into the sky with tears of joy. I said: "Dad, I love you, and there's no doubt you are up there watching. You'll always be with me when I walk these woods."

The rest of my group couldn't believe it. When we talked about it over dinner that night, I kept saying: "Man, I stayed calm for the buck. It was like I was walking in my father's boots for a day."

When I kicked off my boots that night, I thought about the fact that all the boots in our family are the same. My father had bought everyone new boots one day, all the same size and color. Each pair had the owner's name written inside, but the ones I now wore said, "Dad." That was the icing on the cake.

That was probably the most emotional moment of my life.

Joe Caruso
Middleburgh, New York

TAKE YOUR FATHER HUNTING

So much is said today about the future of hunting. Taking children hunting and introducing them to the outdoors is endorsed by almost every hunter. I have two sons and I couldn't agree more with those thoughts.

However, I believe we are overlooking one aspect of our hunting heritage. I'm talking about those who used to let us clean their guns or carry their limit of ducks. They're the ones who taught us the difference between rubs and scrapes, and demonstrated how to tell a good story. If you haven't guessed by now, I'm talking about dear ol' Dad.

He had his hunting buddies, as we now have ours. The only difference is that in many cases, some or all of his are gone. We head into the fields and woods each fall with our hectic lifestyles and the latest technology, while he sits watching the first flock of geese head south and dreams of days gone by. Don't we at least owe him an invitation?

Most fathers won't ask to come along on one of our outings or hunting trips. They don't want to be a burden and get in the way while you're taking all the necessary precautions to get your trophy buck. It might take a little effort on your part, and you might even have to insist that he come along.

Here are a few suggestions for getting your older hunting buddy to spend some time with you. Invite him along on scouting trips, whether it's driving the back roads in late summer to glass fields, or putting up stands in the early fall. Also, there are a lot of conservation areas that offer good dove hunting on opening day. That's an easy way to spend some time afield with the kids and their grandfather.

Another suggestion is to try a game preserve. They are now located almost everywhere, and are open from early fall until late winter. Most offer a variety of

Father and son spending a happy moment in a goose blind.

This blind makes for comfortable, productive deer and turkey hunts for the father-son team.

upland birds, as well as dog rental, and most of these outfits will really try to cater to your needs.

My brothers and I built a blind for our father to hunt from. It has enough room for two people, which helps pass the time when things are slow. He is able to stay out longer, and his time in the outdoors is a little more comfortable. There are many portable blinds that set up with ease, and they work well for deer and turkey hunting.

The next time you head into the outdoors, remember one of the reasons you're out there to begin with. I realize this doesn't apply to everybody, but if you still have the opportunity, "Take a Dad Hunting." He will not invite himself along, so you have to. He won't care if he brings home game, or even fires a shot. What matters is time spent together, rekindling old memories and maybe sharing one more story to retell around a fall campfire.

Mike Winka
Flora, Illinois

MY HUNTING ATTITUDE

Hunters might consider the following techniques and attitudes, much as my father and grandfather taught me:

Never shoot anything you do not intend to clean and eat (yes, that means armadillos too). Never kill more than your family can eat or than you can give away to people who will eat it. At least once, donate an entire deer to a needy, hungry family. Most states have a "Hunters for the Hungry" program. Pass down our hunting heritage to the next generation; these days, they need all the stability they can get.

William Tong
Lufkin, Texas

SPECIAL GROUND BLIND

Getting people of all ages and abilities involved in hunting is important. Whether they're elderly, handicapped or young and fidgety, having a good blind increases everybody's hunting success. Here's how to make a blind that's accessible for just about anybody.

Get eight pieces of 4-foot-long PVC pipe with a half-inch inside diameter. Also buy four PVC corner pieces that will receive three pipes. One hole on each PVC corner will be threaded for a screw-in coupler. Glue the four threaded couplers to the four legs.

The other four 4-foot pieces will be your top rails; they slide in and out of the couplers to put up or take down the blind. Drill two opposite sides to receive clip pins.

Cover the sides with military tank netting or any kind of camouflage netting, and fasten it down with cable ties and the clip pins.

To keep the blind stable, you need four 4-foot pieces of rebar rod to serve as stakes. Drive each rebar rod 2 feet into the ground. Slip the four legs over the rebar. They must be four feet apart. Legs might need to be shortened for some wheelchairs.

John L. Cripe
LeClede, Idaho

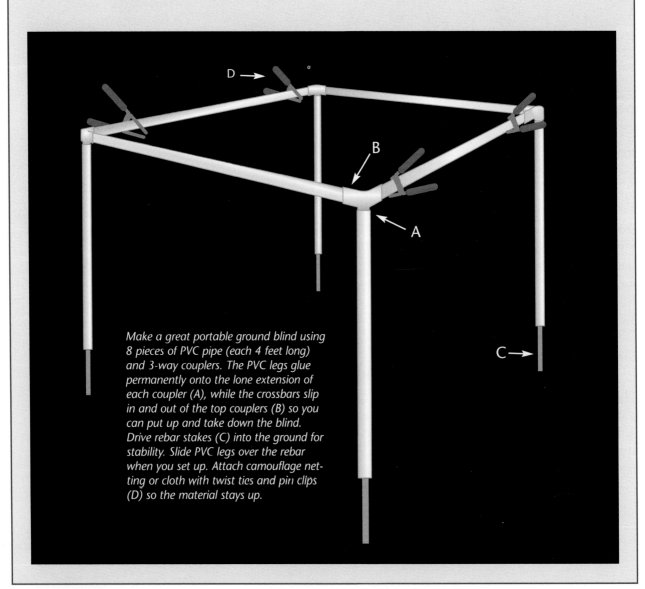

Make a great portable ground blind using 8 pieces of PVC pipe (each 4 feet long) and 3-way couplers. The PVC legs glue permanently onto the lone extension of each coupler (A), while the crossbars slip in and out of the top couplers (B) so you can put up and take down the blind. Drive rebar stakes (C) into the ground for stability. Slide PVC legs over the rebar when you set up. Attach camouflage netting or cloth with twist ties and pin clips (D) so the material stays up.

THE PERFECT HUNT

It was 4:30 a.m., and I was riding in the truck with my two favorite hunting buddies—my dad and my brother Luke. It was cold that morning, maybe just below freezing. We took the dirt road to our duck hunting spot. It's tucked away in the high desert of northern California where sagebrush grows high and trees grow low. This is where wild horses still run free and coyotes howl at the luminous moon.

We had stumbled upon this place while hunting sage grouse a few months before. We were three of the few lucky people permitted to hunt this wary and intelligent bird. As we wound our way down the bumpy road, we had our traditional hunting breakfast of donuts and hot chocolate, except for Dad, who preferred to keep warm with a cup of coffee.

We arrived at our spot and parked the truck on the roadside. We got out quietly, closed the doors, and opened the truck's tailgate. Our dad put on the only pair of waders, because my brother, who was 14 at the time, and I, who was 15, weren't quite big enough to keep a pair up. Instead, we put our rubber boots on over our wool socks. We already had on our layers of clothes, and we grabbed our decoys, guns, ammunition and lunches, then began our rough hike through the lava beds and sagebrush.

The wind was blowing nearly 20 mph as we arrived at the shoreline of a small lake surrounded by brush-covered hills. Dad set the decoys in the shallow water as my brother and I set our things next to rocks not much bigger than bowling balls. Other than these rocks, we were naked of cover. Our father finished with the decoys and we sat down and talked about the wind, which was blowing in our faces, and about the decoys, which were going berserk on the water.

My brother and I were excited to the point where we were about to explode. You see, we had been on a few duck hunts before with our dad, who is an excellent shot and a great sportsman. In fact, he's taught us everything we know about hunting and the great outdoors. Yet my brother and I had never been able to line up our barrels on one of these magnificent birds.

Shooting time came, and from afar we saw the golden glimmer of the butter-like sun. As we watched the ducks fly, we prepared ourselves for a day we knew would provide a great hunt. Waves of birds came in one after another, and our shooting started off a little rusty. But as the birds decoyed into our father's calling, we shot a little better and started hitting an occasional bird.

As the action slowed and we admired our mallards, shovelers and pintails, we glanced at a nearby hill to see a herd of pronghorn antelope moseying down the hill to get a drink of the crystal-clear water. At that moment, I realized it's not the killing of birds that makes a great hunt; it's what you see and who you see it with.

James Jubran
Hudson, Florida

EARS REQUIRE HEARING PROTECTION

When shooting, always use hearing protection. This is important when teaching someone to shoot. It's often the noise that causes a shooter to flinch and fear recoil. The new shooter will enjoy shooting, and everyone will go home without ringing in their ears. Also, don't forget eye protection.

Robert J. Manske
Portage, Wisconsin

GETTING KIDS INVOLVED IN HUNTING

This story is not about how to put meat on the table or harvest a trophy animal. It's about something more rewarding. And it requires little skill and no special formulas or techniques. What can be more rewarding than harvesting a mature whitetail or a wise old gobbler, you ask?

I'm going to talk about introducing children to the outdoors. Seeing the expression on children's faces when they hear a turkey gobble in the wild for the first time, find their first mushroom, or catch their first fish. These are all memories that last a lifetime. Remember a few simple things when introducing children— be they your offspring or someone else's—to the outdoors. Some of these tips should make the experience more enjoyable for both of you.

Many people hesitate to take children into the woods during hunting season, because of safety reasons. But most of the activities that allow you to introduce your child to nature actually can take place outside of most hunting seasons.

The first activity to consider is fishing. Fishing is probably every child's introduction to the outdoors, simply because ponds, streams and lakes are accessible to nearly everyone.

Whatever activity you plan, make sure you introduce children at their own pace and make the sessions short. This lets kids thoroughly enjoy the time spent and makes it easier for you to hold their attention.

One of the easiest ways to introduce children to nature is to set up a bird feeder in the backyard. This gives children the opportunity to view and identify birds and squirrels at their own pace. If you need to brush up on identification skills, or you want children to learn to identify birds on their own, buy an inexpensive book to help guide your efforts.

Another good way to introduce your child to nature: Take short walks in the woods in the spring before new growth emerges. The weather is usually pleasant, and sign such as tracks, droppings and trails are usually more visible. Also, children might be rewarded by hearing a turkey gobble, finding a mushroom, or finding their first shed antler. Again, keep trips short, make sure the children are dressed appropriately for the weather, and make sure they're wearing comfortable boots or shoes.

If you want to take children along to sit in the field or woods, buy a portable blind or build one

To build a better chance of producing a hunter, start a kid out with simple but fun outdoor activities well before he or she is old enough to hunt.

Time is what matters. Just taking the time to be with a youngster in the outdoors will make a difference in his or her life. And maybe yours.

(see page 14). Make sure it's large enough to hold at least two people, and bring a couple of portable stools so a child can sit comfortably. Portable blinds are great because they're lightweight and allow children the freedom to fidget or move around. They even allow the child to enjoy a snack or drink without spooking game. Be sure to set up along the edge of a field or woods, where increased visibility provides a better chance of seeing wildlife.

Finally, bring along a small 35mm camera on your outings. Photos will be cherished memories of your child's introduction to nature, and they will also allow the kids to start their own scrapbook or photo album of their outdoor adventures.

When taking the time to introduce children to the outdoors, keep it simple and let them go at their own pace. The memories and rewards will last forever.

Mark Winka
Xenia, Illinois

TEACH A KID TO HUNT

Take kids hunting! It wasn't long ago that I used to be the one watching and not shooting. Actually, kids can be lots of help. Kids have good eyes. Some of the best hunting buddies are the ones who don't even know what the heck they're doing. They see something that doesn't look normal, and they tell you about it. And, frankly, it usually turns out to be what you're looking for. I am only 15, but have already introduced seven kids to hunting. Some of these kids have been interested, but have never had the chance or the equipment. Also, some of them just didn't realize how fun and worthwhile hunting really is.

Kody Jon Anderson
Fountain Green, Utah

FRAGMENTS OF PARADISE

After weeks of the city, office and artificial light, the draw of the forest at dawn is almost irresistible. It fills me with a delicious anxiety, an excitement reminiscent of a child's haste. When I finally find myself among the trees, and urban humanity is but a hushed din in the distance or forgotten altogether, I am greeted by a simple impulse: to inhale deeply. Long before I load my shotgun or glass the thickets, I savor the fresh air, the anticipation and the incomparable peace of land left primarily in nature's care.

Many of my weekends are spent in the rapidly vanishing woods of the suburb in which I grew up. There, armed only with binoculars, I watch a flock of turkeys feed, a whitetail doze in the sun or a flicker flash through the branches. I absorb the sounds and smells, see and hear what I see and hear when hunting. Yet with a slight shift of my gaze, there comes into view an enormous shopping mall, and thousands of parked cars glisten through the

Gary Hohenberger's friend, Alethea Wojcik, took this picture of Gary and another friend—just hunting for a fragment of paradise.

trees. It is then I realize I have found a tiny fragment of paradise in the woods.

That thought returns to me when I venture afield with gun and knife. The forest is a place full of magic, and any hour that I can spend among such abundant beauty is blessed. Even if I do not leave with the gift of a squirrel or a deer, I am rewarded with a bounty of memories. In the forest, there are stories around every bend.

Flattened grass and scattered feathers recount the pheasant's final encounter with the fox. Nipped branches betray how anxiously last year's fawns await spring. That hole in the oak has been home to many lives over the years, though the tree itself is long dead.

Out of gratitude for the deer's supple lines, the creek's coolness or the chickadees' friendship, I gather whatever trash someone else has left lying about, picking up rusty shell casings and foam cups, filling my pockets with the carelessness of others. I know that my conscientiousness cannot keep up with the disrespect and neglect dealt our public lands, but I feel better leaving those few acres better than I found them.

And when I close my eyes at night after a day's hunt, I still see the orange disc of the sun through evergreen boughs, and the sticks and leaves continue to crunch beneath my feet. I carry those images long after the game meal has passed through me, and long after the season has closed. They dim and fade, vivid only in dreams, until I visit another fragment of paradise.

Gary F. Hohenberger Jr.
New York, New York

PRACTICE YEAR-ROUND WITH PELLET RIFLES

Too many hunters squeeze off a couple of quick rounds from their rifles before deer season and consider themselves ready for the season. But practice is everything, and when taking a good deer requires a somewhat difficult shot, we sometimes miss or we pass up the shot because we don't have confidence that we can make a clean kill.

John Schapansky, 15, is shown here with his first white-tailed deer. The doe was taken with his .30-06 Remington Model 700 at 100 yards. He made a clean shot through the heart.

John and Abe practice year-round, shooting box after box of .177-caliber air rifle pellets on their farm. They practice shooting long and short shots, quick shots and even shots taken in poor light conditions … all mimicking the reality of a real hunt. We all know it's rare to get the chance to hunt in ideal conditions.

Practicing with an air rifle improves critical shooting skills and also provides a great opportunity to get other kids involved in shooting and hunting. Kids love to shoot and, as experienced hunters, we owe it to the next generation to spend time training them.

Abe Schapansky is happy with three ruffed grouse taken with his 20 gauge.

Dave Schapansky
Abbotsford, British Columbia

A Very Special Turkey Season

For the third year in a row, I had not drawn a permit for one of Michigan's early spring turkey seasons. But if you don't draw an early season you can purchase a permit that can be used almost anywhere in the state in late May.

But late May in Michigan means heavy foliage, much rain and lots of bugs. The turkeys have already been chased a full month, making them call-shy, decoy-shy and, in most cases, mostly done breeding. Little did I know the season would be the biggest learning experience—and most successful turkey season—I ever had. The biggest lesson I learned was to always keep a positive attitude.

I love calling and hunting wild turkeys. My father-in-law, Gilbert, drew a tag for the first season, so I took a day off to call for him. He had been watching the turkeys' patterns, and knew they came through his woodlot every day. When opening morning came, we stepped out the back door and were greeted with 30 mph winds and a cold front.

After setting out our decoys, we realized the turkeys had lockjaw. In the afternoon, the winds died down and it warmed up. At 2:30 p.m., we returned to the same spot. After about 30 minutes and several calls on my box call, I turned in time to see four big jakes approaching the decoys from behind us. We watched as they walked in and strutted around. Gilbert's shot dropped a fine 18-pound jake.

He thanked me and said it was all the trophy he needed because he believed in taking what the good Lord offered. The fan and 5½-inch beard hang on his living room wall.

While waiting for the late season to arrive, I learned my friend Bob also had a permit for the late season.

The first Saturday of the late season found Bob and me sneaking down the lane behind his dad's house at daylight. As we walked up to a large barley field at the end of the lane, Bob grabbed my arm. Just over the hill in the middle of the field, a turkey flared its

Any spring turkey you get—jake or gobbler—is a good one and makes for a special season.

wings and jumped into the air. Seven toms were in the field chasing around, fighting and spurring each other before walking off.

Bob and I made a wide circle and sat down at the fence 60 yards from where we had seen the toms. I crept out and set one hen and one jake decoy. Shortly after, I started calling with the diaphragm call, followed by a couple of gobbles with my shaker. After 10 minutes, three red-and-white heads peek over the hill.

With a few soft calls on a push-pull call, in they came: three jakes side-by-side in three-quarters strut. On the count of three, Bob and I shot, dropping two fine jakes. My bird weighed 19½ pounds and had a 7-inch beard. Bob's jake weighed 18 pounds and had a 5¾-inch beard. Bob and I were both happy.

On my way home, I stopped by my Uncle Bill's. He also had a late-season permit, but wasn't having any luck. Next to my father, Uncle Bill is the most influential person for me in hunting and fishing.

I asked him if he wanted to try hunting in the morning. When he said yes, I knew it would be a great opportunity to help pay him back for all those years of fun, learning and support he showed me.

The next morning we set up on a field of corn stubble east of his house. After several minutes of calling, we had a hen walk within feet of us. She then came through the fence and walked to the decoys. I could tell Uncle Bill was enjoying the hen's show. Later that day I called Bob to see if we could try for a bird on his father's farm.

The next morning, Uncle Bill and I set up on the field where Bob and I had shot our jakes. I called, got an answer, and soon a huge bird stepped into the field about 300 yards away. He strutted on the hill for about 20 minutes. When I called, he would take a few steps toward us and stop again. This continued until the bird was about 60 yards away.

But he had no beard! He weighed 25 pounds if he was an ounce, and he also had a beautiful tail with light cream-colored tips. Uncle Bill looked at me like I was crazy when I told him the gobbler had no beard. I gave Uncle Bill the binoculars so he could see for himself. Then a hen came into the field and called the beardless tom into the swamp.

I told Uncle Bill tomorrow would be the last day I could hunt, and talked him into coming over to my

Late-season hunting can be your best hunting.

house to hunt the next morning. He said he would be over around 8 a.m., and we agreed that would be as good a time as any because we weren't seeing birds until after then anyway.

The next morning, as Uncle Bill pulled into the driveway, it started to rain. He told me he had seen three toms in a small L-shaped field around the corner from my house. When I said I had permission to hunt that field, Uncle Bill's face lit up and I could see a sparkle in his eye again. We headed down the lane on my ATV, then began our stalk.

It was raining hard. As we walked slowly through a 40-acre woodlot, I could see the field growing closer. When we were in gun range of the edge, Uncle Bill set up next to a small tree. I pulled out my shaker call and let out a long gobble. Much to my surprise, an answer came from behind us! I called again, and another gobble roared from behind us.

Suddenly, I realized we got turned around in the woods and had sneaked up to the wrong field! So we angled toward the field where we heard the turkeys gobble. As we drew within sight of the field, I shook the gobble call and got an immediate answer.

Peeking into the field, I spotted three birds way up by the road. I started calling with my mouth call and one bird gobbled. After a couple minutes, the tom started walking across the field, going away from us. I realized I shouldn't have used a regular hen call on these overhunted toms. When I used a gobble, the bird stopped.

I reached into my vest and pulled out a push-pull call to imitate fighting purr sounds. I watched the birds as I did the purring, and every time I did it, the biggest of the three strutted and gobbled, and then took several steps toward us. I kept calling and he continued slowly working his way across the field. When the tom reached 40 yards, I told Uncle Bill he better get his gun up. When the tom was at 30 yards, Uncle Bill said a small tree wouldn't let him move his gun for the shot. I slowly reached up and pulled the sapling over so he could move the gun. At about 20 yards, the bird was in full strut and facing us. I could see a long, heavy beard and full, beautiful fan.

He strutted and drummed a few inches closer. I told Uncle Bill to take him. As I turned my head back and looked at the tom, Uncle Bill fired and the bird fell. As I walked out to make sure it wasn't going anywhere, I realized just how big the bird really was. Uncle Bill walked up and, for several minutes we didn't say anything ... we just stood there looking at the bird.

Later, the bird weighed 25 pounds, with a thick $9\frac{3}{4}$-inch beard and $1\frac{1}{8}$-inch spurs. I would have never thought such a bird could be fooled in May. Uncle Bill's turkey made a perfect end to my turkey season. What really made it special was sharing it with good friends and family.

I did a full cape mount of Uncle Bill's bird and gave him a photo of us the day of the hunt. It made me feel good to give Uncle Bill something back for all the great years he had given me.

I'll have a hard time beating that season, but you can bet one thing: I will have a different attitude when I hunt southern Michigan's late turkey season from now on.

Bruce Lautenslager
Albion, Michigan

TEACH KIDS THE RIGHT HUNTING ATTITUDE

This is a story about attitude. I had gone dove hunting with a friend for my second time. My children—Melissa, age 10, and Daniel, age 8—went with me for their first time. I am a hunter safety instructor, and my children sometimes attend the classes with me. We do discuss hunters' attitudes. During this weekend of dove hunting, I showed my children you don't always have to win and kill game to have fun; just be safe.

I was borrowing a friend's gun for the hunt, so I had to ask questions to become familiar with the gun and its use. Then I sat and watched the birds to learn to identify doves from the other birds. My daughter sat with me and my son sat with my friend, who is an experienced hunter. My daughter was picking up on everything much faster than I was. When I felt confident about identifying the birds, I decided it was time to try to shoot one. In all of the excitement, I forgot to load my gun. It sure is difficult to shoot a bird with an unloaded gun! I always kept my muzzle pointed in a safe direction.

My next mistake was forgetting to take the safety off. Finally, I safely made it through all of the obstacles, but could not hit a bird. My children observed and commented that I practiced all of the safety tips we teach in class, but the birds were safe when Momma was hunting.

They also learned that hunting really can be fun even if everyone else gets something and we don't. I know because their question was this: "When are we going bird hunting again?"

Dove hunting is a great family activity to enjoy together, and valuable lessons can be learned.

Laura Butcher
Irving, Texas

HUNTING PARTNERS
ENHANCE THE EXPERIENCE

The enjoyment and success of any hunting trip is enhanced by the right companion—someone who shares your interest in the outdoors and has respect for the wildlife pursued. A person like this is a real treasure. On the other hand, the wrong partner can make for an unpleasant experience and might even be hazardous to your health.

Having hunted with many people over the years, I have come up with a list of attributes an ideal hunting partner should possess. He or she should:

- **Be safety conscious.** Your sidekicks should be people you trust in the woods. Their firearms will always point in a safe direction and be unloaded before reaching your vehicle or camp. The safety will be on at all times right up until the shot is taken. I check the guns of new hunters every so often during the hunt. Your partners should also be aware of anything in the line of fire when shooting at game. Your life is in their hands. Check them out.

- **Play by the rules.** Your hunting companions should respect game laws and limits, and hunt only during the legal season. They should respect posted property lines and never litter. Good sportsmanship is essential in promoting our hunting tradition.

- **Be on time.** There is nothing worse than having a gobbler roosted and then miss the fly-down because your partner overslept. I will not wait for someone and, if it happens regularly, that partner is history! Missed connections and wasted time afield ruin the best plans.

- **Exhibit woodsmanship.** Good partners should be able to read animal signs and be familiar with the habits of their quarry. Knowing your way in the woods and being able to read a compass is a big plus. Building an emergency shelter and knowing basic first aid also comes in handy.

- **Show a good, positive attitude.** Ideal hunting partners will think positively and be willing to hunt hard in all kinds of weather. They will climb mountains, wade rivers and stay in the woods all day. You hear no complaints or excuses, because they enjoy the outdoors completely and look forward to each day afield with renewed excitement.

- **Have patience.** The ability to remain still and wait out quarry puts more game on the table than anything else. After making a difficult deer drive over rough terrain, you want to find your partner still on watch and in position for a shot. Patience is an absolute must! Any movement by your buddy while calling in an elk or longbeard can make for a long ride home.

Along with the above qualities, it would be nice if your partners field dressed your game as well as theirs, and transported all game taken back to camp. It would also help if they packed a big lunch, carried all your gear and offered their vehicle (with a full gas tank, of course). But I guess we can't have everything. Nobody's perfect!

I am fortunate to have the ideal hunting companion. We have hunted together about 18 years now, and he possesses all the qualities listed above. He's also a crack shot and a hard hunter. It seems as though he blends into the woods and becomes a part of it. He is my son.

Michael Williams
Poultney, Vermont

LIFETIME MEMBERSHIPS = LIFETIME FRIENDSHIPS

Being an avid turkey hunter, I wanted to bag a Merriam's gobbler. One April, I hunted in the Black Hills near Lead, South Dakota. Our group arrived from different parts of the United States with high hopes. That quickly changed when an April blizzard dumped 4 feet of snow. What a disappointment for a turkey hunter who had traveled all the way from West Virginia!

A state worker named Lester Kopel was plowing snow from the highways. Lester and I started talking about hunting. Lester is a Life Member of the North American Hunting Club. He told me I could come to his place and hunt sometime.

That snow might have been a blessing for me. Les gave me his address and phone number. We kept in touch and a few years later I returned to the

Black Hills to hunt with Lester's help. I was joined by another Life Member, Roy Bowers, and Member Wayne Williams.

We flew from Virginia to Rapid City, South Dakota. There we rented a car and drove to Whitewood to meet Lester and Sandy Kopel. They were great hosts and did everything possible to make our hunt a success. Les, Roy and Wayne bagged toms. But the Merriam's once again was not to be mine. Because of other hunts and commitments, I did not get to return for a few more years.

After we had arrived and bought our licenses, it was only 2 p.m. We would still have time to check Les's area for turkeys.

Life Member Kenny Crummett, of West Virginia, with a South Dakota Merriam's gobbler.

Life Member Lester Kopel with his contribution to the hunt.

We made a 4-mile trip by ATV to an area where Les had seen gobblers. We set up and started calling. Within minutes we got a response, and a gobbler walked straight to my inflatable decoy. It seemed unreal to have my first Merriam's gobbler on the ground at 6:30 p.m., just 4½ hours after arriving in South Dakota. What a turnaround from my previous Black Hills hunt!

Saturday before dawn we made the 4-mile ATV ride to our area, and soon heard gobblers on all sides of us. After calling until 7 a.m. with no response, we moved and heard a gobbler. We got within 150 yards and set up. The gobbler answered our calls but moved down the ridge away from us. We then returned to our first location and scared some gobblers that were strutting in the small meadow. After lunch at Lester's house, we took a break to let the gobblers settle down.

We arrived back on the mountain about 4 p.m. and set up near a pond where we had seen a big gobbler that morning. After 30 minutes of calling, a flock of eight to 10 gobblers moved through the pines in our direction. Lester whispered for me to shoot the lead gobbler. At 30 yards, I put the sight on its neck and squeezed the trigger. Les shot the second gobbler. The

others scattered. My trophy weighed 21 pounds, 2 ounces, and had a 10½-inch beard!

After a few days of sightseeing, we decided to try filling Les's second tag on Tuesday. After arriving at our area, we heard at least five gobblers. Within 30 minutes, two gobblers were strutting about 75 to 80 yards from us. Then a hen came within 10 yards of us and fed for at least 20 minutes. She then moved toward the gobblers, who paid little attention. After using a box call to entice them, I saw them moving across a small knoll, where they spotted our decoys. They kept strutting as they closed the gap. When the lead gobbler got within 40 yards, Les's shotgun roared and he had his second trophy. This one weighed 19 pounds and its beard measured 7¾ inches.

The NAHC has many benefits for its members, but meeting another member like Lester creates a lifelong friendship. Being able to experience such a memorable hunt is the Club's greatest benefit.

Kenny Crummett
Sugar Grove, West Virginia

SHARING THE HUNT

A WOMAN TAKES UP THE BOW

I just started hunting recently, but I always thought bowhunting was a challenging sport and that someday I would like to hunt for deer. My husband has been bowhunting for about 18 years, and I envied the time he spent in the woods enjoying nature. So once our children were mostly on their own, I decided to tackle the sport. I also liked the idea that it would provide quality time for Craig and me—something that we could share in common.

I've had some challenges along the way. I started that May by trying to draw my son's bow. I couldn't even pull it back. For three weeks, I lifted weights to build up my muscles. But I still couldn't draw the bow. So I continued to lift weights.

Finally the day came when I could draw the bow, but I had a long way to go before I was ready for the woods. With the encouragement and guidance of my husband, I spent many weeks shooting at targets.

Craig also taught me the terminology of bowhunting, from the bow itself, to planting crops for deer, and deciphering deer sign in the woods. I spent the rest of the summer climbing treestands and shooting from the nine stands Craig put up in his father's 40-acre woods. When opening weekend arrived, I was ready for the woods. Knowing I was only accurate from 20 yards, my next challenge was to get a deer within that range.

My only hope the first year was to see deer. I didn't care if they were does or bucks. I wouldn't be picky. Because of the strategic locations of all my husband's stands, I saw a lot of deer. Unfortunately, nothing came within shooting range until Craig and I went north to Pembine, Wisconsin. Craig and I were within sight of each other, and we used two-way radios so we could talk, and he could help guide my shooting.

A big doe walked within my self-prescribed shooting range. I drew on her, but Craig could not see her because she was standing by a tree. I decided not to shoot, because I was unsure of the shot and the doe had her fawns with her.

Even though deer seldom came into my shooting range, I got into the woods every chance I could. It didn't matter to me that I hadn't shot, because I was seeing deer and I was enjoying the outdoors. I saw foxes, turkeys, grouse, squirrels, birds, skunks, beautiful sunsets and even a magnificent rainbow! Being in the woods in autumn is great. I hadn't realized that leaves falling could make such a loud noise as they hit the ground. And the colors were awesome.

Then, on a brisk November day, the first day of our vacation, I got a big surprise. While my husband was checking his treestands, he saw a huge buck in the woods. He came home and asked if I would like to get my hunting gear on and see if the buck was still in the area. Of course, I said yes!

As luck would have it, the buck had not moved from the spot where Craig had seen him. We both crept up on the buck and Craig told me to shoot at him. At first, twigs were in the way, so I had to reposition myself for a clear shoot. Then I thought I wasn't within my shooting range, but Craig told me to put my 20-yard pin on the buck and shoot behind his shoulder. I drew my bow, paying attention to my anchor spot, sight triangle and target spot. I said, "Well, here goes." My arrow seemed to travel through the air at such a slow pace, but it finally got to the buck.

Craig said, "You hit him in the perfect spot!" The buck ran off, and within a minute we heard a big crash.

Now we just had to track him. The blood trail was good, and in only 5 or so minutes, we found the buck. It was a 9-pointer and weighed about 180 pounds.

I was ecstatic and in shock! I then tried to field

Beth Charles with her buck.

dress the buck, but I cut the stomach, so Craig took over and finished the job. What an exciting time!

I realize if I hadn't received help from an excellent hunter, my husband, that this would not have been possible. It's a moment I will never forget.

I encourage more women to get involved in bowhunting, because it's a great experience. A lot of patience and work goes into bowhunting, but the payoff can be wonderful. Plus, it's something special you can share with your spouse. I'm hooked for good.

Beth Charles
Green Bay, Wisconsin

FOCUSING ON THE SEARCH

According to the dictionary, "hunt" means to search for or pursue game. If we keep the focus of hunting on this meaning, we have a much greater likelihood of enjoying a successful hunt.

It seems many hunters equate hunting with shooting. Shooting is just one small aspect of the hunt. How we approach our actual search for game is of the utmost importance. Our planning and strategy for determining the ifs, wheres, whens, whats and hows of the hunt add to the anticipation, satisfaction and pure enjoyment of the actual hunt.

The hunting permit is merely a license to search for game and legally take the game if the situation allows. We have no right to any game simply because we possess a license!

In our conversations with fellow hunters and with those who do not hunt, it would be wise also to focus on the searching aspect, rather than the shooting aspect, of hunting. That focus might be helpful for placing hunters in a better light among our acquaintances. We hunters all firmly believe there is nothing wrong with hunting and that hunting is a wholesome experience. However, as we know, not all people share those thoughts.

Dan Leuenberger
Lincoln, Nebraska

SUCCESSFUL STRATEGIES, LASTING MEMORIES

As the son of an avid sportsman, I began to hunt white-tailed deer at age 12 with my father. I didn't realize it then, but I was about to build an enormous store of knowledge and memories that would last a lifetime. What an awesome experience, harvesting such magnificent trophies in reward for doing my homework by scouting, picking good stand sites and, most of all, practicing safe hunting practices. The pictures and the deer on the wall are nice, but what's more important are the memories; they are like a video playing in my mind.

Over the past 20 years, I have been fortunate to harvest about 40 whitetails. Some hunters might believe a trophy must score high enough to make the record books. I believe every deer is a trophy. Whether it's a doe, a small buck or a multi-tined brute—it's a trophy in my book.

I'm proud to give all the credit for my success to my father. I will never be able to thank him enough for everything. He brought me up to respect nature, make good decisions and follow all conservation laws.

During the past 20 years, I have been successful for several reasons. My father always joked around and nicknamed me "Lucky Lewie." If five of us went hunting for the day, I always seemed to be the lucky one. But it wasn't luck that made me so successful. I could give some credit to luck but, to be honest, it was the strong sense of pursuit that was instilled in me when I was young.

During many hunting seasons, I traveled to different states to hunt whitetails. During most of the out-of-state trips, I was pressed for time and had only one day to scout and another to hunt. I had to make sure I followed three main strategies: walk until I found a heavy concentration of deer sign—droppings on the ground and trees rubbed and ground scraped during the rut, if possible. Two of my largest trophies were taken with this one-day strategy. I scouted until I was satisfied that I knew the area. Then I placed my stand according to the wind, the sun and the scrapes.

You might be thinking, "sun direction?" A friend once taught me to always place my stand facing north, if possible. The reasoning is that the sun will never be directly in your eyes if you face north, and that might help in many situations. Although you might not always be able to do this, try to face your stand north as often as possible.

One important tip: If you're a bowhunter and you have already drawn your bow on a deer and just can't hold any longer, stay at full draw and lower your bow. Rest it on your thigh at full draw. This technique will relieve the burning in your arms and maybe buy you another minute!

Another lesson I've learned over the years is to pay attention to what's going on around you in the woods. For example, many times when I hear a bluejay screeching, I see a deer within 20 minutes. Nature's signals can alert you to many things.

The success of your hunt will depend on your strategies and on being in the right place at the right time. If you do your homework, you should succeed.

I'm 34 years old, and I've been disabled the past two hunting seasons. I'm now unable to enjoy my most precious time of the year, and I miss how excited I always got each fall. But all is not lost. I might be able to overcome my disabilities and return to do some hunting. If not, I have every memory of each hunt stored in my mind. I can close my eyes and almost relive each hunting moment.

Good luck to you, and I hope you're as fortunate and successful as I have been to have so many great hunting memories.

I would like to dedicate this story to my father, Lewis Barney, and a great friend, Keith Oliver. I've hunted with both for years. God bless you and safe hunting.

Lewis Barney Jr.
Belle, West Virginia

PASSING ON THE HUNTING HERITAGE

One great aspect of hunting is being able to teach your children about the outdoors. Giving back some hunting knowledge to the next generation is a great feeling. I love my children dearly and want to share the outdoors with them.

I want them to see beautiful sunrises on the open marsh, hear the great horned owl and turkeys just before dawn, and see the woods and swamps come alive in the late afternoon hours. I want them to feel the cool wind on their faces and anticipate the arrival of ducks on the wing or deer on the hoof. I want to share the natural world with them and teach them respect for the land they hunt and fish, so as they grow older they will be good stewards of the land. I hope they will get that special feeling, deep in their soul, every time they go afield.

When they grow older, if they decide not to hunt, they will understand hunting and respect nature enough to know hunting is a necessary part of wildlife management.

I once experienced a duck hunt with my father and my 4-year-old son, Tyler. Three generations shared a natural bond. I cannot describe the special feelings I got on that magical day. Then, after deer season ended, I took Tyler on a squirrel hunt that he enjoyed.

Remember a couple of things with first-time hunters: The younger the child, the shorter the hunt should be so they don't get bored. Keep the weather in mind, because you want the child to enjoy the outing without getting cold or wet. By making the hunt fun, you might create a lifelong hunting partner.

Take a child hunting, and both of you will be better for it. If you don't have children of your own, I'm sure you know a child who would love to learn what the world of hunting is all about.

William Trout Jr.
Bridgeton, New Jersey

Father and son.

Grandfather and grandson.

HIGHLIGHT OF THE RABBIT HUNT: LUNCH BREAK

When my family and friends take our beagles rabbit hunting, we have a noontime tradition of roasting rabbits for lunch. We normally hunt bottomlands, and are usually miles from the truck when lunchtime arrives.

So each person carries part of the lunch. One carries a 2-pound coffee can with a zip-top bag of water inside, as well as a small bag of coffee. Another carries cornbread or biscuits. Another carries small cans of beans and a big red onion. Each hunter carries a small container filled with half seasoned salt and half black pepper, plus a metal or plastic cup.

Wherever we happen to be at lunchtime, we prepare a safe fire site and build a campfire. We cut long-forked green sticks, and thread each rabbit onto the stick so it is spread wide and flat. We make deep cuts every 2 inches over each rabbit, and give it a heavy coating of the salt and pepper mix. Next we roast the rabbits over a medium fire for about 40 minutes or until little juice is dripping from the meat. While the rabbits cook, we boil the coffee in its can.

Whether you're old or young, nothing is better than sitting around a warm fire with good friends, good food and a much-needed rest for the dogs and ourselves. When we finish lunch, we put all trash in the can and pack it home. The only sign we have been there is the ash pile and the logs where we sat.

In some cases, the game you hunt can also be what's for lunch.

Gary W. Hart
Edmond, Oklahoma

ALWAYS BRING A CAMERA

Make all your hunting adventures last a long time. Bring a camera! Today's technology makes purchasing a good 35mm camera relatively inexpensive. You can get a good weather-resistant camera for less than $300. I recommend a weather-resistant camera because we all know you'll hunt in wet, damp or sloppy conditions.

I have a Pentax Zoom 90WR that takes great pictures and has all the functions and features I need, even an infrared remote control so I can take pictures of myself when nobody is around.

Another tip: Take photos in addition to, and other than, kill-shot pictures. Take pictures of your camp and hunting area, other wildlife, your hunting buddies and hunting dogs. Buy a photo album just for hunting pictures and enjoy, remembering all aspects of the hunt.

William Trout Jr.
Bridgeton, New Jersey

BUILD YOUR OWN GUN SAFE

Not everyone has $1,000-plus to spend on a gun safe. But you can build an effective, child-proof gun safe out of an old freezer for less than $100! Usually a person can get an old freezer from an appliance store for no charge. They have to dispose of them, and are grateful for someone to take them off their hands.

I started with a 16-cubic-foot model that had a bad refrigeration unit, but the cabinet was like new. I gutted the refrigeration unit and shelves, then I lined the cabinet with half-inch oak plywood, using deck screws to secure it to the cabinet. Next, I built shelves out of pressboard and secured them with glue and screws. I notched the gun rack to accommodate 10 guns and lined it with black felt. I applied a coat of polyurethane to the entire wood structure, and added a "golden rod" safe heater to prevent rusting.

The finished safe.

I secured the door with a strong clasp and padlock. I modified the exterior door hinge screws by drilling out the screwdriver slot to prevent anyone from removing the door.

The entire project took about 10 hours of work.

The safe can be secured to a wall (from inside) to prevent anyone from moving the cabinet.

The variations one might apply are whatever your imagination can conceive. Another variation might incorporate a lazy Susan gun rack inside to easily remove and display your guns.

I also recommend trigger locks, and storing ammunition in a different location.

David B. McDonald
Lockport, New York

Open-door view.

BUILD YOUR OWN GUN SAFE
PARTS LIST

1	16-cubic-foot freezer	free
1	4-by-8-foot sheet of ½-inch oak plywood	$29
2	10-inch by 48-inch by ¾-inch shelving (pressboard)	$12
	felt material	$5
	deck screws	$4
	wood glue	$3
	padlock	$6
	clasp	$6
	12-inch "golden rod" safe heater	$30
	Approximate total cost	**$95**

GIVE YOUNGSTERS SOMETHING TO CROW ABOUT

Many adults, myself included, make the mistake of cutting a child's hunting teeth in the deer woods. For some reason, we think a child will sit quietly on stand for hours. We soon realize 15 minutes or less is about all most children can handle before needing to announce they are cold, bored and uncomfortable or ask loudly, "When will the deer come?" … all accented with a great deal of squirming.

When my oldest granddaughter showed interest in hunting, I decided I would not repeat the mistakes I had made with my children. Emma was 5 years old when she begged to go hunting with me. This time, I was prepared. With my hard-learned knowledge that children are human noise machines, I handed Emma a crow call. I taught her the basic three-note, "caw, caw, caw" call, set her out on the back deck, and told her, "When you get a crow to come to your call, we'll go hunting."

Every time Emma visited my home, she went out on the back deck and practiced her crow call. Then one evening, Emma came running into the house all excited.

"Omi, Omi! I called in some crows. Come watch!" We went out on the deck, and Emma threw out her best calling. She was soon greeted with a flock of crows yelling back at her. I gave

Crows are noisy. Kids are noisy. It's a perfect hunting matchup!

Emma a big hug and told her, "You're my hunting buddy now. Let's go get them!"

The next day, I decked Emma out in camo and we headed to a nearby field. I set Emma under a tree with three foam pads under her for comfort. She began to call, and soon a nosy crow came flying by to check us out. That was its last flight.

Emma yelled with joy and excitement, running up to the downed crow—her crow. You would have thought I had shot a trophy buck. We both danced around our kill. A great bond was born that day; not just the bond of grandmother and granddaughter, but of huntress and huntress.

Emma is now 7, and we have perfected our crow-hunting skills, calling alone or in unison to create the noise of fighting crows. I know that with every outing, Emma is learning more about the woods and the animals in it. I know when Emma is ready to handle her own gun or pursue bigger game, she will let me know.

Give crow hunting with a child a try. The expense is small, the need for noise is satisfied by the calling, and the time spent with each other in the field is priceless.

Richilde Glennon
Bennington, Vermont

COSTUME PARTY FOR THE KIDS

When hunting geese over decoys, I use magnum decoys to cover my twin 12-year-old girls. To allow them to see better, I take my Dremel tool and cut half-inch-wide slits 8 inches long in the decoy's back so they can see.

Christie Berg
Logan, Kansas

KIDS' SHOOTING BOX

HUNTING TIPS

When my kids were younger and not yet ready to handle firearms, I let them shoot BB guns. As they got ready to hunt, I cut out photos of deer, elk, boar and turkeys, and pasted them on a homemade BB trap. This gave the youngsters a chance to practice shooting at "big game."

The BB trap was a cardboard box filled with balled-up newspapers and some tiles from a drop ceiling. We could "hunt" for hours without leaving the backyard!

Bobby Dolan
Hollywood, Florida

For would-be hunters, a few magazine pictures can make target practice fun and interesting ... more so than plinking at rings and a bull's eye. Plus, you can start teaching some shot placement skills.

Getting kids hooked on shooting BB or pellet guns is a great first step to hooking them on the shooting sports and hunting. Their confidence grows with every session and will transfer to the field when that time comes.

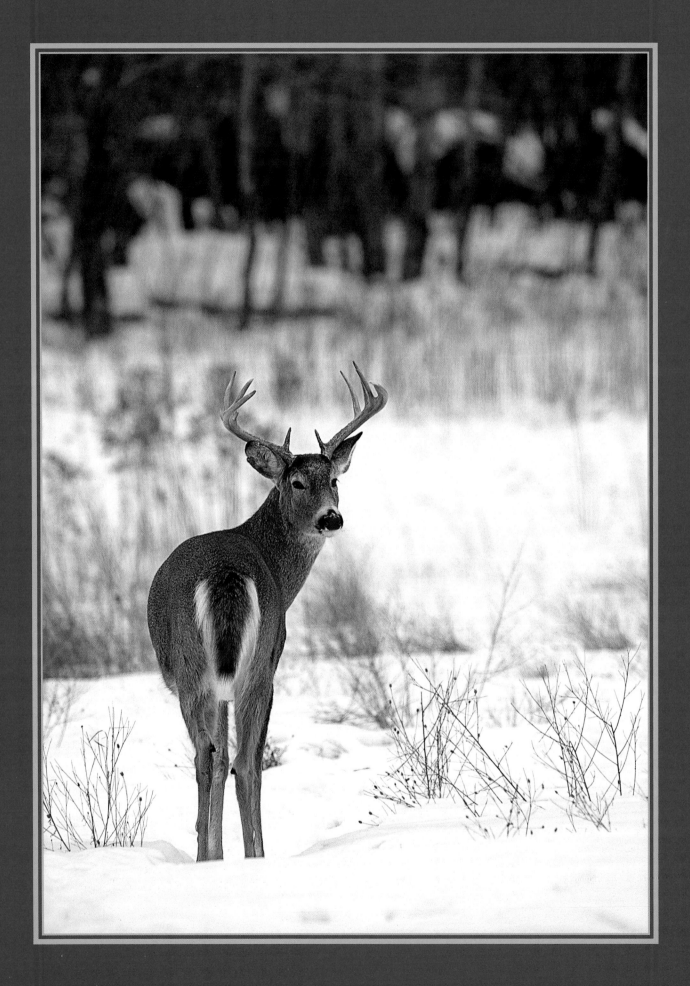

DEER

Just who is a deer hunting "expert"?

It's easy enough to label yourself as such, publish some stories, make a video, write a book ... generally proclaim your vast storehouse of skills.

But who *really* knows deer and deer hunting? NAHC members. See what they have to say about the *how* behind the deer hunting we all love so much ... and also the *why*.

MY FIRST BUCK

The morning was clear and cold, and a couple inches of snow had fallen overnight. Snow squeaked beneath my boots as I headed for my favorite deer hunting area. A stiff breeze touched my face, making my cheeks and ears tingle. The wind was directly from the west, which would be ideal for my still-hunt.

Because the rut was on, I was hoping to ambush a buck. Deer seemed to be traveling heavily through this part of the woods.

The 6-pointer stood up, stretched, looked around … then started walking toward the author.

by on his daily quest for food. Sunlight filtered through the hazy sky, brightening the woods. In the distance, I heard swans migrating south.

Coming up to a small ridge, I found a trail with fresh tracks. A couple of deer had passed through earlier. I decided to follow the trail upwind. At a small creek, I paused beside a tree.

As I scanned the woods, I saw movement ahead. Coming straight at me was a buck. The deer was already 50 yards away and was coming at a fast trot, his nose to the ground and his tail up in a jaunty way. Evidently, he was following a fresh doe track and I was standing almost on top of it. I tried to move away from the trail, but the buck was already too close. I held still, hoping he wouldn't see me.

The buck kept coming until he was only 5 yards away. Looking straight at me, he sniffed the air. He didn't seem afraid, but he knew something wasn't right. The buck had an 8-point rack, with main beams out to the tips of his ears.

He started to move around me. He sniffed the ground. Apparently a doe in heat had urinated there. Then he pushed his nose into the snow, he lifted his head up and curled back his upper lip. Shaking his head, he turned and walked away.

Unable to shoot, I watched him go. If I had been a couple of yards to the side of the path, I might have had an easy shot.

I slipped through the barbwire fence and into the timber. I started my stalk, easing along the small game trail. The early morning conditions were perfect. A slight breeze blew fresh snow off the branches, making enough disturbance to cover most of my noise and movement as I took one slow step at a time.

Ahead of me, a fox squirrel shuffled along in the snow, digging nuts. Unaware of me, he passed close

Feeling I had blown my chances, I was startled when a smaller buck appeared! This deer had a bead on the first buck and wanted to scare away the trespasser. With his ears back and his back humped, he walked stiff-legged after him. The first buck wasn't worried about the smaller buck's tough act, for he kept walking unhurriedly away.

I began to wonder if I should follow. But the smaller buck turned and came back, heading toward me. I stepped behind a big oak tree. The buck kept coming until he was 20 yards away. Brush prevented a shot. The buck stopped near some small pine trees and bedded down less than 20 yards away.

I tried to sneak closer to an opening in the brush, so that when he stood up I would have a better shot. The buck stayed bedded for about an hour, chewing his cud. He was always on the alert, listening to every little sound.

I sneaked as close as I dared, taking a step only when the wind blew snow from the branches to cover any noise I made. By then the buck had stopped chewing his cud and was licking his back and legs. After five minutes of cleaning himself, the buck slowly stood up and stretched, looking around as he started walking my way. Dry-mouthed, I watched as the buck headed for an opening 15 yards away. Walking slowly, he stepped into the opening and stopped broadside.

With hands shaking, I raised my Bear recurve and pulled the string back. As the base of my thumb touched my cheek, I instinctively released. The arrow flew true, hitting the buck behind the left foreleg. The buck took off running full speed, and was quickly out of sight. I heard him crashing through brush, and then everything was silent.

With shaking hands and trembling knees, I replayed the shot in my mind. I was pretty sure my shot had been good. The blood trail was easy to follow. As I hurried along, I came to my blood-covered arrow. The cedar shaft was broken in half. I picked it up and kept following the trail, my eyes glued on the tracks. I walked within 10 feet of the buck, which was lying dead on its side.

The beautiful animal that only a few hours before had been free, wild and very much alive was now lying at my feet. Kneeling down, I lifted its head.

The antlers had three points on each side, but because this was my first deer after many years of hunting, antler size mattered little.

The buck had been a fighter. His face had scratches and scars. Two of his short tines were broken off. I placed my tag on one of the antlers and started to field dress him. I thought about the past six years, and of how many hours I had put in trying to get a deer, never getting a shot until today. As I looked at my 6-pointer, I smiled. This moment had definitely been worth all the time and effort.

Aden D. Miller
Windsor, Ohio

VASELINE KEEPS STANDS QUIET

My portable treestand had a noisy seat. Every time I moved, the cloth rubbed loudly on the stand's metal parts, scaring away game or alerting it to my position. I solved the problem by putting Vaseline on a rag and wiping the metal underneath the cloth seat. The sound disappeared. Vaseline has little odor and lasts a long time. It works!

Hal Kettunen
Grand Marais, Minnesota

EASY DRAGGING

To ease the chore of dragging your deer out of the field, hook the front legs over its head. Then place your drag rope over the head and hoofs. This way, the deer's front shoulders don't hang up on trees and brush.

Mark Stender
Casco, Wisconsin

HUNTING THEN, HUNTING NOW

I remember "the old days." I was too young to hunt, but opening days were big at my home. The day before the season, most of the guys would show up at my parents' house with a gun, a small bag of gear, and big hopes. At night, they would play penny poker until whenever. I had an 8 p.m. bedtime.

In the morning, I would smell the bacon, eggs and coffee. I would wake up in a smaller room than where I fell asleep, meaning more hunters had shown up late and bunked in my room. I had to step over sleeping bodies on the floor. People were sleeping in the attic too. It was a full house. Before dawn, they would be out in our driveway drawing maps in the dirt with a stick to see where everyone was going. One of my favorite things was learning the crazy names of all the treestands: the Old Oak Stand; Horseshoe Trail Corner Stand; and my personal favorite, Leaning Crotch Stand. There was also Joey Hoe's platform stand, which was big enough to sleep two.

Before leaving, they did their equipment check: gun, ammo, knife, compass and license, and nothing

more. Then out to the woods they'd go for their morning outdoor nap. But some of them actually hunted. Everyone was back by 11 a.m., and then they snacked on their lunch for a few hours and took another nap. Then they went back out to hunt until dark.

We always knew a blowing horn meant someone got a deer. It was simple and fun. Yes, those were the good old days.

Hunting today ... boy, how things have changed. Everyone shows up at my house now. Dad is gone, but I feel him hunting with me on every trip. There's no time for penny poker. I'm lucky if the hunters show up by midnight. It seems like everyone has to work more these days. The house fills up and now I get to displace my own kids to make room.

No more maps in the dirt. My driveway is paved and my wife won't let me draw chalk maps on it. I print out a topographical map from my computer for everyone, which shows our trails and stands highlighted and labeled.

These guys have too much stuff: three gear bags and two guns each. Some do their equipment checks before they leave: radio with headset, GPS receiver, cell phone, compass, maps, raingear, portable deer decoy, electric socks, binoculars, three flashlights, chair, portable treestand, climbing sticks and the list goes on until each guy weighs 900 pounds. Now we bring a bag lunch so we can be out from dawn till dark.

Too many sneak work out to the woods with them. I'm worried about them. I keep telling them to relax and enjoy the hunt and nature. They just laugh. Sometimes I miss the good old days. I still go out with just my gun, ammo, a hot seat, knife and compass, and hope in my rush that I'm not forgetting the rest.

Those are just some of the differences between then and now.

Matthew Ippolito
Wurtsboro, New York

ONE-SHOT PRACTICE SESSIONS

When daylight allows, take one shot with your bow every morning before going to work. (This is in addition to your regular practice.) Take your time and make the shot count. If your practice shot didn't hit where you had wanted, you have all day to think about what happened. (Did you torque the bow? Jerk the shot? Commit some other error?) This will also help you realize how important continued practice is, and, consequently, you will become a more proficient shooter. Remember: In the real world, you will probably only get one shot, perhaps for the entire season.

Tom Storer
East Granby, Connecticut

20 HINTS FOR WHITETAIL HUNTERS

After more than 40 years of hunting whitetails, I believe these 20 hints will help make any hunting experience more productive and enjoyable. But always remember that a deer doesn't trust his ears or eyes as much as he trusts his nose. If the wind is wrong, none of this will help much. So that's the basic, overriding instruction: Always try to hunt with the wind in your face.

Some of these hints are old, some are new, some I borrowed and some I just knew! I hope they bring more whitetail hunting success your way.

1. Always wear knee-high rubber boots when hunting whitetails.

2. Baking soda is excellent for washing hunting clothes.

3. Baking soda can also be put in boots to control odor.

4. Never step on deer trails, and be careful where you put your hands when crossing a fence.

5. Change hunting clothes often and hang them outside to dry after you've washed them.

6. Try to have enough stands to choose from, so you can switch depending on the way the wind blows.

7. Keep clean clothes in a plastic bag, away from odors.

8. Never smoke, fill your truck with gas or shop while wearing your camouflage clothing.

9. Hoist your pull-rope into the stand after climbing up, because the rope has your scent on it and it waves around.

10. Change directions when going to and from your stands, so you can't be patterned easily.

11. Never slam doors when leaving your parking spot to hunt.

12. If possible, walk into your stand by wading through a creek, stream or river.

13. Carpet all stands to quiet them, and always climb into and leave them quietly.

14. We all know about clean clothes, but don't forget to also deodorize your pack, bow and other accessories.

15. To keep from sweating, don't wear your heavy clothes on the way to your stand; carry them, and put them on after you've arrived.

16. Bowhunters: Never hunt without a face mask or face paint, and always cover your hands.

17. Glasses, watch and camera lenses all shine. Keep them covered—or in a pocket or pack—as much as possible.

18. Make sure your bow and stand are quiet.

19. Some cover scents work, some don't.

20. Use rubber gloves whenever possible.

Kal Sears
North Platte, Nebraska

CONTROL YOUR SCENT

To help control breath and body odor, hunters can take activated charcoal tablets and/or chlorophyll tablets. Both of these supplements are available at health-food stores or from mail order nutritional-supplement companies. These tablets are particularly effective when you've eaten spicy foods or have been smoking cheap cigars at camp.

Tim Grieneisen
Brockway, Pennsylvania

CALLING WHITETAILS
THE ART OF SNORTING

All white-tailed deer hunters want an edge to get that big buck a little closer. I'm amazed that many hunters have not tried snorting at bucks, because it's not necessary to purchase fancy calls to do so.

The first buck I snorted at was the first buck I killed with a bow. I was in a treestand just inside a small woodlot, next to a soybean field. It was late October on a beautiful, sunny morning. About 10 a.m., I looked to my left and behind me and saw a small doe. Immediately behind her was a 6-point buck. Both deer entered the soybean field and headed on a diagonal to the northeast.

I wondered what I could do, if anything, to get them to come to me. With nothing to lose, I tried snorting at them. I had never tried snorting at deer before, so not only did I not know how I would do it, I did not know when I should do it, how many times I should do it, or how the deer would react. But what the heck. So I made a circle with my hand by touching the tip of my thumb with my index finger, took in every bit of air I could force into my lungs, and then gave a mighty blow through the circle I had

Once your snorts have drawn his attention, he knows where you are. Don't snort again unless he loses interest and starts wandering off.

made with my hand. The reaction to my snort was immediate. Both deer stopped cold and looked back toward the woods and me. After a couple of minutes, they started walking away again. So I gave another mighty snort, and again they stopped.

We played the game a while, and the buck finally reached and entered the woods. I shut up completely. I knew I had his attention, and chances were good he would come in my direction. Within two minutes, the deer walked within 10 yards of me, and I shot my first buck with a bow.

The next year, I got my chance to try it again. A buck walked within 15 yards, and I had my first Pope and Young Club whitetail. Sometimes, snorting provides that little extra enticement to make a buck curious enough to come closer. Snorting doesn't work every time, just like grunting doesn't work every time. But snorting works some of the time, and only when done correctly.

Here are a few tips about snorting at bucks:

• When you snort, take as much air into your lungs as you can hold. When you blow it out, blow it out in a quick short burst.

• Make a circle with your thumb and index finger, and bend the rest of your fingers in a cup shape to line up with the index finger. I think blowing the air through the circle and past the rest of the hand gives the snort a more realistic sound.

By the way, I do this with gloves on.

• When you blow out the air, do it with an attitude. Think mean and mad when you do it. You are trying to imitate a buck with a nasty disposition. You must do it with attitude to make it sound realistic.

• Never snort at a buck when he is looking at you. Wait until his attention is somewhere else. You want him to know the general direction the snort came from, but you do not want him to pinpoint your location.

• Do not snort excessively. Snort to get his attention, and if he stops and looks or comes your way, do not snort again unless he puts his head down or starts to walk away. You have his attention.

• Use snorting with other types of calls. Try grunting first, and if you get no reaction, snort at him. You'll be surprised what a deadly combination this makes. Besides, if you have already grunted at him and gotten no reaction, what have you got to lose?

Try snorting at bucks. It will increase your chances of success, and give you another tool to use in trying to harvest your next white-tailed buck.

Ned Gibson
Swartz Creek, Michigan

WEAR LATEX GLOVES TO YOUR STAND

Whether you are walking to and from your stand or are scouting in the woods, wear latex rubber gloves to help control your scent. These gloves will keep you from leaving scent where you move limbs out of the way or touch anything else accidentally. The gloves come in boxes of 50 or more and are cheap. They are also a must for field dressing game.

Vincent Butts
Tecumseh, Michigan

Latex gloves keep your scent off your hunting area.

BEATING BUCK FEVER

Over the years, I've read countless articles about bowhunting whitetails. Yet I seldom see much advice on how to deal with buck fever.

I don't mean the radical cases, where a guy forgets to draw his bow or pumps five live shells out of his shotgun. But what about that big 8-pointer last year that you missed by shooting too low? You knew he was farther than 20 yards, but you used the 20-yard pin anyway.

Every year, hunters go out with high-tech equipment and punch bull's eyes at 40 yards. But on the first deer at 15 yards, they draw and release without taking time to focus on the yardage or their anchor point. Obviously, that results in a bad shot or a clean miss.

One thing I've learned is that there is no cure for buck fever, but if you keep a few things in mind, you can live with it. Here's how.

• **Calm.** If possible, don't hurry. The more you hurry, the less clearly you think, leaving you more prone to screwing up.

• **Yardage.** It's always a good idea to put out range-markers. I've lost a couple of nice bucks on misjudged yardage.

SHOOTING REST FOR TREESTANDS

Use an extra tree step to help you make a shot and get better shot placement on deer and other big game when hunting from a treestand or even from the ground. This is a good way to use old or bent tree steps that are not safe for climbing. Here's one important tip: Don't rest your barrel directly on the tree step or your shot will go high. Place the gun's forend on your hand on the step when shooting.

William D. Trout Jr.
Bridgeton, New Jersey

A screw-in tree step makes a steady rest. Place the gun on your hand or a finger, to cushion any "bounce" that might happen.

• **Anchor.** Perfect form on the target range doesn't mean anything if it's not put to use in the woods. That's why I stress spending days on the range before each season, so it becomes second nature to draw smoothly, anchor solidly, hold and release.

• **Focus.** While it's fine to count the points and estimate the spread while a buck is working his way in, once he gets close, focus on where your arrow should go. I wish I had a dollar for every time a hunter shot through a deer's antlers! But that's where hunters often focus.

• **Release.** A clean release is imperative. Bad releases cause many, many misses.

As hunters and sportsmen, it's our responsibility to make quick, clean kills. It's inevitable that we make bad shots now and then, but if we can remember these few things, we can reduce our miscues.

The next time your hands get clammy, you feel short of breath, your heart pounds like it's going to jump out of your chest, and your knees are shaking so badly you almost can't stand up, try to remember these steps: Calm, yardage, anchor, focus, release.

Christy Schmucker
Quincy, Michigan

STAY ALL DAY

As a New York state whitetail hunter, it took me a few years of learning the hard way to realize how important it is to stay in the woods all day during the rut.

I hunt with a bow and a 12 gauge shotgun. Once a doe starts moving around for food and begins attracting bucks, you never know when a buck will decide to sneak in. All thoughts of patterning deer should be dropped, except for trail networks and escape routes. Bucks start traveling all day in search of receptive does. Typically, the busiest times are early morning, another hunter's lunch time, and minutes before sunset. Pack water and a quiet lunch. Let other hunters go to lunch and push an unseen trophy to you. Keep still and don't let any deer see you first.

When deer are near, control your breathing so your breath clouds aren't obvious. I find that exhaling through my nose doesn't cause as much moisture to be visible. If a buck comes in silently from behind until he snaps a branch directly over your non-shooting shoulder, don't move! Stay motionless. If he doesn't know you're there, he will pass through and offer a shot.

Mark McGrath
Warsaw, New York

Stay out and hunt all day. Some of the best success comes just either side of noon.

BAD WEATHER WHITETAILS

Some of my best deer fell on some of the worst days to hunt that can be imagined.

In bad weather, the whitetail's senses are limited. When the wind is blowing and it's raining or snowing, all three of the deer's defenses are hampered. The wind takes away a deer's nose and hearing, and confuses its eyes. Rain deadens noise and drives scent to the ground. Snow makes deer stand out, and a heavy snow limits what they can see while reducing the noise you make.

Deer bed in protected spots during rough weather. They also move around more to find better areas if they get uncomfortable. Both of these habits work to your advantage if you know the area in which you're hunting.

Check any protected spot out of the wind, or walk a ledge or ridge while watching the protected downhill side. Gullies, wide gorges and swamps with heavy cover hold deer in rough weather. Standing corn is also a good place in farm country. The idea is to see deer before they see you. Most deer I have taken in this manner were facing into the wind and looking downhill. Their heads look like radar sweepers when they try to watch all directions at once on windy days.

Move slowly. Match your movement to the movement of the woods or cover. You don't want to move so fast that you don't see deer. Slow down

He is out there when the weather is bad, and in many ways he's more vulnerable. So get out there and hunt.

when you spot a deer, and move only when it's not looking your way.

Using this tactic, I was able to sneak within 50 feet of a nice buck whose antlers are now on my wall. Be ready as soon as you're within range. If a deer senses something is wrong, it will come out of its bed 30 feet to the jump! Get your sights on him at this point, because deer will often stop within range to look for what spooked them.

Watch out for more than one deer. You might only see one, but there could be more. This can work for or against you. I once had a buck jump out of his bed during muzzleloader season, but he didn't stop within my self-imposed shooting range. However, a huge doe stood up from her bed and just stood there looking after the buck. She never saw me. On the other hand, it's just as easy for an unseen deer to spoil your stalk. If one deer spooks, everything usually goes with it.

When that happens, try a wide, sweeping stalk to the downwind or crosswind side. Much of the time, even a herd of deer will not go far in rough weather. This is especially true if they aren't sure what spooked them. I once bumped eight does three times before getting a clear shot. Each time I came in from a different side and caught them watching their back trail. The total distance covered was less than a

Let snow and cold keep other hunters out of the woods. You? You should be there hunting the unpressured deer.

quarter-mile. If a deer scents you, though, all bets are off. You might as well look for other deer.

Bad-weather hunting is ideal for a two-person team. Keeping 200 yards away from your partner lets you bounce deer between your partner and you. Or one of you can sit in cover while the other pokes around, trying to get deer up and moving. Both hunters must wear blaze orange or another bright color to keep track of each other.

I always wear a red or hunter orange hat and hunter orange for safety, no matter what the law requires.

Even though you might not see another hunter on really bad days, be careful to identify your target and be safe yourself. Good luck and good hunting.

Gordon Betts
Cazenovia, New York

HUNT WHEN IT'S DRIZZLING

Almost all hunters I know shy away from drizzly, rainy days.

They think a light rain or drizzle will keep deer, elk and moose from moving about to browse and feed. Nothing can be further from the truth. My most successful hunting days have been such days. I believe deer are smart and can easily pattern hunters. On overcast, drizzly days, deer hear very little noise from vehicle traffic or from human traffic because most hunters stay in bed or at home. Deer know they can move around more freely, because no hunters are out there.

Another advantage with drizzle or rain is that it muffles or obliterates the sounds of a person walking. It also helps minimize your scent.

Such conditions might make things challenging for your comfort, but they're just part of everyday life for deer, elk and moose. They're out there 24/7, regardless of the weather.

Glenn Heisler
Bainbridge Island, Washington

STILL-HUNT WITH A CROSSWIND

Hunt with a crosswind whenever possible. Deer will bed with their backs to the wind and look downwind. By moving crosswind, you have a better chance of approaching a deer's blind side. Use binoculars, even in thick cover.

Ronald Andrus
Manteo, North Carolina

MAKE YOUR OWN EUROPEAN MOUNT

Preparing a European mount for your wall does not involve a mysterious or complicated process. The items you need are: a kettle large enough to hold the base of your antlers, a sharp knife, one gallon of common household bleach, a saw and brown shoe polish.

STEP 1

Cape out the head. If you have not done this before, have someone show you how, or do some research in hunting books. A little research might be worth your while, because you can often sell a carefully removed cape from a good-sized buck to your taxidermist for a premium price.

STEP 2

Submerge the skull in a kettle of clean water. Heat to boiling, then simmer until the meat separates easily from the bone. This might take as long as four or five hours. Some doomsayers worry that the bones will fall apart if they are boiled too long. My experience shows that boiling until the

Simmer until the meat separates from the bone.

meat easily separates from the bone presents no problems, and the final process sets the bones and teeth firmly. Make sure the skull is fresh and unspoiled. But even boiling fresh game meat produces odors that some find offensive. If the smell bothers you, boil the skull outside or add spices such as rosemary to the water.

STEP 3

Remove the flesh from the bone. Most of it will come off easily. What is left can be cut away with a sharp knife. Don't worry about little bits of flesh left behind. The bleaching process will take care of those remnants.

STEP 4

Saw off the back of the skull. This accomplishes two things: First, it allows you to clean out the brain area. Second, it gives you a flat surface, making it easier for you to hang your mount later.

STEP 5

Set your boiled, cleaned skull into a clean, empty kettle. Carefully pour in one gallon of bleach. Add cold water until the skull is covered just below the burrs on the antlers. You can put blocking under one edge of the kettle so the bleach water will touch less of the antlers. (Note: You do not want bleached antlers.) Let the mount soak in the bleached water for 12 to 24 hours. A gallon of bleach might sound like a lot, but in my experience, this method produces excellent results.

Bleach the skull but not the antlers.

The skull comes out a beautiful white, and the bleach removes the small bits of flesh you might have missed in step 3.

Step 6

Let the skull dry overnight. When dry, the skull will be whiter than when first removed from the bleach water. It will look and smell clean. Any teeth that were loosened during the boiling process will set tightly during this drying.

Step 7

If the bleach whitened part of the antlers, darken with brown shoe polish. Be careful not to get any shoe polish on the white skull.

You're done! This method is fast and easy, and produces a handsome, rustic-looking mount. You can drill a hole in the skull and mount it on the wall as is, or fasten the skull to a plaque

Darken any bleached portions of the antlers.

Stephen Dodge
Noxon, Montana

The final product—a rustic trophy that is handsome to behold.

USE BINOCULARS TO TRAIL DEER

The technique I use for following difficult blood trails involves a good pair of low-power binoculars. My first experience with this method involved a Pope and Young whitetail in Kentucky several years ago.

Knowing I had made a decent shot, but being unable to follow the blood trail, I tried a technique I had thought about but had never used. I stood beside the last drop of blood, focused my binoculars at about 10 feet and began searching each leaf in a circular pattern around me. Each leaf looked like it was under a magnifying glass! After expanding the circle to about 12 yards, I spotted what looked like a quarter-sized drop of blood to the side of the trail the deer had been following. It took me a few minutes to find that blood with my naked eyes. I had to go back to the binoculars at least three times to identify the correct leaf. The blood drop was actually smaller than a pencil eraser, but it got me headed in the right direction again.

After following the trail another 250 to 300 yards, and having to resort to my binoculars several times, I finally found my buck. He was my first 10-pointer, and I never would have found him without the binoculars.

I have since used this method many times with good results. I believe the key is to use low-power, wide-angle binoculars that can focus on objects at short distances. The binoculars must be easily steadied and be easy on your eyes. It takes patience to search each leaf, but the rewards are worthwhile if you love your sport and your quarry.

Calvin Almond
Pinehurst, North Carolina

According to the author, binoculars work wonders for close-up blood trailing work.

 # BLOOD-TRAILING TIPS

USE HYDROGEN PEROXIDE

Pouring hydrogen peroxide into a spray bottle gives you a cheap blood trailer. Spray it around the foliage on the forest floor. The peroxide will foam immediately upon touching any bit of blood, which will allow you to distinguish blood from red spots on leaves.

Mike Weiss
Reese, Michigan

Hydrogen peroxide foams when it hits blood, making a blood trail easier to follow.

ANALYZING BLOOD & HAIR

Watching a deer's reaction after you shoot is the best way to determine where your bullet, slug or ball hit. But hair at the scene, as well as the blood trail leading away, also lends evidence as to what kind of a hit you're dealing with, and whether or not you should press on hard, go cautiously, or wait a little while before following the deer. The evidence isn't always pretty, but neither is the prospect of losing a deer.

HAIR

Coarse, hollow, brownish gray, tips not black: Stomach.
Dark, long, coarse, hollow, black tips: Spine.
White, coarse, hollow, curly: Navel.
Dark, short, somewhat coarse: Foreleg.
Fine, white, silky: Inside hind leg.
Very long, coarse, wavy, dark on top or snow white below: Tail.
Long and dark guard hairs, possibly graying: Heart.
Stiff, grayish black, curly, coarse: Brisket.

BLOOD

Bright, pink, bubbly, possibly sprayed to side: Lung.
Bright red, not bubbly, might also spray: Heart.
Bright red, dribbles into tracks: Muscle/Leg.
Dark red, not bubbly: Liver/kidney.
Flecks of bright pink tissue: Lung.
Flecks of green or yellow: Gut.
Bone fragments present: Leg.

Tom Carpenter
Plymouth, Minnesota

TRACKING BLOOD

Did your deer's good blood trail just stop? Deer will sometimes backtrack and jump off to the side like a rabbit. Look to the side toward thick cover. If the deer is tired and wants to lie down, it will pick a site that offers cover and a good view of its back trail.

Ronald Andrus
Manteo, North Carolina

BE A TURKEY WHILE STILL-HUNTING

I hunt whitetails exclusively by still-hunting, and I have found a way to make this method productive. The two requirements are to have turkeys present in your hunting area and to be able to use a diaphragm turkey call.

Still-hunt as you would normally, trying to be as quiet as possible. Obviously, don't break large branches or wear noisy clothing. Also, be sure not to allow your footsteps to sound "human" in dry leaves. By this I mean putting your foot down flat and allowing the footsteps' crunching to be drawn out. This is alarming to deer, because all animals' footsteps are "sudden."

The key is to use your diaphragm turkey call every few moments. Cluck, purr and yelp, trying to sound like a feeding turkey. Kee-kees and kee-kee runs are also effective, because there are lots of young turkeys in autumn. Always be sure to call before moving into an area where you expect to find deer. That way, if you make a noise, the deer

The sounds you make while hunting through the woods are not unlike those a turkey would make. Let out a cluck, purr, yelp, kee-kee or other turkey sound every once in a while and you may be able to get within range of an otherwise suspicious buck. But for safety reasons, don't use this method when the fall turkey season is open.

will not be alarmed, because they expect noise from the turkey they heard calling.

You cannot call too much, because a flock of turkeys can make a lot of noise. I do not try to sound like a feeding flock. I only use the call to cover any noise I might make. You must move slowly, and be sure not to expose your silhouette against any skyline. Of course, hunt into the wind or with a crosswind. Binoculars are a must, allowing you to spot bedded deer from a distance.

I started using this method several years ago after watching a bedded doe and two fawns. I could hear turkeys coming from the other side of the ridge. The doe contentedly chewed her cud and never looked behind her as the turkeys crossed the ridge and fed past her at 20 yards. I have used this trick to get within 40 yards of a bedded deer, and have shot several deer in their beds.

Of course, don't use this method if the fall turkey season is open.

Although I've never tried it for anything but deer, I believe this technique would also work on elk, mule deer or any other animal living where turkeys are present.

Steven Shaffer
Cambridge, Ohio

TURKEY CALLS CAN FOOL DEER

When still-hunting for whitetails during dry conditions, imitate natural sounds that occur in your hunting area. Turkeys and people sound similar while walking, so I use a mouth diaphragm call to yelp and cluck occasionally while walking. This allows me to get much closer to deer without being discovered.

For safety reasons, don't use this method in areas where deer and turkey seasons run concurrently.

Robert Holmberg
LaPine, Alabama

TOSS STONES TO IMITATE ACORNS

When acorns are falling and you are hunting from a stand, carry some marble-sized rocks. If a deer holds up out of range, softly pitch some rocks into the air above the limbs to imitate falling acorns. The deer will come seeking the fresh acorns to eat.

Sam George
Brunswick, Maryland

Drop a rock, attract a hungry deer.

MONITOR MAST CROPS

When hunting mast crops in the early season, realize there is a time lag from when the mast drops to when the deer find and eat it. For example, you might discover that deer are pounding the acorns. However, the beech mast dropped later and you might find the nuts lying untouched all over the ground. Rest assured, deer will soon discover the beechnuts and abandon the oak groves for the plentiful beech bounty. The trick is to locate the area of the deer's next food source before the deer arrive, and hang stands there.

Tim Grieneisen
Brockway, Pennsylvania

GEAR BINS KEEP EQUIPMENT HANDY

One way I stay prepared for the long New Jersey deer season, which starts in October and goes through the end of January, is to pack a plastic bin with extra gear to keep in my truck. This gear includes camo clothing, raingear, extra socks and gloves, sweaters, shirts, hats, extra batteries, knife and spare flashlight. I also pack an extra pair of rubber boots, rope and other accessories. I've had two bins for the past few years. My buddies laugh at all the gear I have in the bins, but I'm prepared for just about anything.

William D. Trout Jr.
Bridgeton, New Jersey

The author is always ready to go at a moment's notice.

USE GREEN TAPE TO MARK TRAILS

To mark trails to and from your deer stands, use light green surveyor's tape instead of blaze orange tape. When illuminated with a flashlight beam, the light green tape shows up much better than blaze orange tape. During daylight, the green tape won't be as obvious to other hunters, thus reducing the risk of giving away your special hunting spots.

Terry Murray
via e-mail

BEST TIME FOR SCOUTING

The best time to scout for bucks is the week after the season. Walk your hunting area and note where you jump or see deer. These are the areas deer flee to when pressured. If you hunt these areas the next season, deer will come to you as hunting pressure increases.

Sam George
Brunswick, Maryland

SIGHTING-IN MADE QUICK & EASY

To sight in a rifle without a bore scope, use a large target with a good backstop (for safety), and put a small mark in the center. Use sandbags for a good rest, hold steady, aim and shoot at the mark. Then, with the gun unloaded, put the crosshairs on the bullet hole. Making sure you steady the gun so it can't move, adjust the scope until the crosshairs are on the mark in the center of the target. Shoot again and fine-tune as necessary.

Robert J. Manske
Portage, Wisconsin

Make sighting-in easy with the author's simple process.

THREAD TIED TO ARROW MONITORS WIND

If you want to keep an eye on the wind yet make little or no movement, tie a 2- to 3-inch thread to your arrow shaft right behind the broadhead. This way, you won't have to keep moving around to work a spray bottle or a powder bottle to check the wind direction. The thread will be a wind indicator right before your eyes.

Samuel Hunt
Capon Bridge, West Virginia

A thread lets you gauge the wind at a glance.

STAY WARM IN THE LATE SEASON

I do a lot of late-season bowhunting, and a good way to stay warm on cold December or January days is to take an old sleeping bag along to your stand. After you're in your stand, step into the bag and zip it up as far as you can. Put your safety strap around you and the bag, and fold the bag down over the safety strap. I have stayed on stand all day and kept warm. You will still be able to stand up and shoot your bow.

Andy Yoder
Middlefield, Ohio

FIELD-DRESSING SUGGESTION

When field dressing a deer that you must drag a long distance, do not break the pelvic bone until you get where you are going. Leaving the bone intact will make the animal easier to drag and will expose less meat to dirt and debris.

Sam George
Brunswick, Maryland

TO STAY WARM, FOCUS ON YOUR FEET

When hunting in winter, dress warmly. Good hunting clothes are worth the money, especially footwear. Nothing spoils your day in the woods more than wet or cold feet. For those whose feet tend to sweat while walking, try powdering your feet with cornstarch before putting on your shoes. It helps wick away the moisture. It also neutralizes foot odor.

Aden Miller
Windsor, Ohio

LET THE BARREL STAY A LITTLE DIRTY

Many people sight in a gun and then take it home, clean it and oil the barrel, including its interior. The next time it's used, the first couple of shots will be off the mark, often a little high and to the left. I like to clean my gun, then take three practice shots to ensure the gun is sighted in. Then I just use gun wipes to clean the outside only, leaving the bore as is so it shoots the same when I'm hunting.

Robert J. Manske
Portage, Wisconsin

Don't hunt with a spiffy-clean barrel.

PRACTICE ON A DEER SHAPE

Having been a hunter for 50 years, I've had the opportunity to coach and train my wife, four children, neighborhood kids and seven grandchildren. After the bull's eye portion of a sighting-in session is completed, I use a deer-sized cardboard target that shows a deer's anatomy so I can stress the kill area. This is a great training aid and encourages a new hunter to concentrate on the vitals. I use the targets the next summer for archery practice.

David L. Wooduff
Sand Creek, Wisconsin

INEXPENSIVE BOW TARGET

For an inexpensive bow target, I use flattened boxes held together with duct tape. Use enough boxes to make the target about 6 inches thick. When the target becomes shot out, simply slide a few more flattened boxes down the center of the target. I have never had a pass-through with this target. Besides being cheap, this makes use of cardboard that might otherwise go to waste.

Daniel E. Burkowski
Oakland, Michigan

DOG LEASH HAULS GEAR

Once secured into their stand, treestand hunters should practice safety by hoisting their gear and unloaded guns with a line. I used a ball of string for years, but this needed to be wound up, and it often became a knotted mess. Sometimes it even became a hazard by getting tangled around my feet.

Then I began using a retractable dog leash as my hoist line. It remains tangle-free, with no line to manually wind up. As I pull up line, it automatically winds up! The device fits into my pants pocket or it can be hung on a nail by its handle grip. Give it a try, and enjoy a safe and satisfying hunt.

Tim Barrick
Carlisle, Pennsylvania

Fido's leash can assist you in your deer stand.

CASTING FOR DEER

If you're hunting the edge of a field or food plot, you can practice your casting skills and distribute scent at the same time. It seems odd to pack my rod and reel on a hunting trip, but this method really does minimize human scent and disturbance.

Start by using heavy line (20- to 30-pound test) and fill a bait-casting reel with 200 yards of line. Next, tie on a 1- to 2-ounce egg lead sinker and a deer tarsal gland soaked in your favorite lure. Add a second 1- to 2-ounce sinker. After you have practiced casting with this system, head to your stand. When you arrive, stand at the base of your tree and cast in several directions. The bait is applied as you reel in.

Vincent Butts
Tecumseh, Michigan

Fishin' for deer can be fun.

TOOLS FOR ENSURING A CLEAR SHOT

Have you ever set up scent-posts in the predawn darkness, and then when the sun comes up, you realize you don't have a clear shot from your treestand? Here's what I do: I put a band of reflective tape or a few reflective tacks above my treestand, on the tree, at my eye level. When I get to my hunting area in the dark, I shine a flashlight up into the tree. If no branches are in the light beam between me and the reflectors, then I know I have a clear shooting lane. This trick saves a lot of wasted time!

Bob Stayduhar
Braddock, Pennsylvania

A "HIDE IN YOUR STAND" IDEA

I found a great hunting site in open hardwoods where a portable treestand is the only answer, but I always had a problem creating a backdrop to hide my profile. Here is the solution I came up with: Take a piece of chicken wire (with about 2-inch holes), a 2 x 4, and 3 short bungee cords. Wrap the wire around the tree at the height you will sit, and secure the wire snugly with the bungee cords. Next, cut several pine branches and insert them into the chicken wire to create a backdrop to hide your profile. I have used this method for several years and have found that it works very well.

Doug Waterman
LeRaysville, Pennsylvania

TOUCH THE EYE TO BE SURE

I know two hunters who loaded still-living deer into their pickups and were driving down the road when the deer "woke up"! Neither hunter had checked to see if the deer were dead for sure, and—obviously—neither had gutted the deer before loading them. Another guy shot a deer, left the woods, got his pickup and drove to the deer. When he grabbed it to load it in, the deer jumped up and ran off. After four hours of trailing, the deer still couldn't be located.

Another hunter I know shot a deer, ran up to it and put his gun down. When he grabbed the antlers to admire them, he found he had a double handful of mad deer. Seems the bullet had hit the buck high on the head, striking the antler and knocking the deer unconscious for a short time.

A lot of hunters assume their deer is dead when it's on the ground and not moving. Some hunters might poke a downed deer in the hip or ribs, and if it doesn't get up, they assume it's dead. The most reliable way to tell whether an animal is dead is to touch its eye. If it has even a spark of life left, it will involuntarily blink. If it is dead, the eyelid will not move.

Glenn Heisler
Bainbridge Island, Washington

LATEX GLOVES KEEP HANDS DRY

Wear a pair of latex gloves under your wool or cotton gloves. This helps keep your hands from getting wet, which helps keep your hands warmer. The gloves also come in handy for reducing the risk of leaving behind scent when setting scent bombs, preparing a drag rag and making a mock scrape. And after a good hunt comes together, wear the gloves when field dressing your deer.

Ryan Stewart
Cincinnati, Iowa

Latex gloves aren't just for doing dishes any more.

SCOUTING THREAD

To monitor deer usage of a trail in an area you're not hunting at the time, tie a piece of sewing thread across the trail and check to see if it is broken when you leave.

Sam George
Brunswick, Maryland

Let some thread be your eyes while you're away.

LOW-DAMAGE WAY TO TAG EARS

Some states require hunters to tag their deer through an ear. Most deer that come into my taxidermy shop for mounting have large cuts in an ear, which makes it difficult to repair and look good. A tagging solution is to carry twist-ties. First, poke a tiny hole into the edge of an ear using a knife tip or the pin of your license holder. Then push a twist-tie through the hole and attach your tag. This easy tagging method saves your taxidermist a lot of trouble trying to fix a cut, and it makes for a better-looking mount.

Jeff Stroka
Big Run, Pennsylvania

EASY DRAG SYSTEM

To make a handy dragging system, start by cutting off a 6-inch piece of a good-sized wooden rod, like that used for closet rods. Next, drill two holes about two inches apart near the center, and then push the ends of a 6-foot rope through the holes and knot each one. Just form a noose over a buck's antlers with the rope and drag.

Ronald Andrus
Manteo, North Carolina

GATHERING SCENT IN THE FIELD

When hunting, carry a small plastic bottle and syringe. When field dressing animals, use the syringe to remove urine from the bladder. This is a great cover or attractant scent for bucks or does, and it's free.

Use a syringe to collect your own pure deer urine.

Sam George
Brunswick, Maryland

DEER HAIR MAKES A GOOD COVER SCENT

Here is a tip I picked up from my father years ago, before anyone came close to making a product to cover your scent and make you smell like a deer. You will need a good set of electric animal clippers or shears, such as those used on horses and sheep.

Shave the first deer you come across, whether it's yours or (with permission) your friend's. Here's how.

Hang the deer with its head down, then lay plastic sheeting underneath. Start shaving from the hind quarters (top) to the head (bottom) as close as you can get to the skin. Continue this until you have shaved the entire deer. I don't shave the legs because of their many scent glands. Avoid shaving blood-soaked hair, because it might cause an alarm response.

Now place all the hair into plastic bags with your scent-free hunting clothes, and place the bagged clothes in plastic tubs. This not only helps

Play barber on a deer, to help you get your next one.

cover your scent, but will attract deer to you. Because deer are social animals, they will want to know who the new guy or gal is in the neighborhood.

Don't try this tip if you're allergic to deer hair!

Vincent Butts
Tecumseh, Michigan

BUTCHERING SECRET: EASY-OFF LEGS

All members of the deer family have two joints in all four of their knees. When removing the lower half of the leg, most hunters use a saw to cut the joint, or they cut off the leg on a bone. But a sharp knife is all you need to cut off the lower leg on all four limbs. Look just below the top joint and you'll find a spot called the butcher's joint. Only tendons and ligaments hold the joint together. Make a cut across the front of the joint to expose the tendons, then slice through them with your knife. The lower leg will fall away. With a little practice, you can find the butcher's joint every time and quickly remove the animal's lower legs.

Glenn Heisler
Bainbridge Island, Washington

FIND YOUR DEER QUICKLY

Keeping track of the direction your deer goes after you shoot can sometimes be confusing once you get down from your treestand. My family has found it helpful to leave a blaze orange item on a limb or the stand to provide a visible reference point back to where you shot from. Also, before getting down, take a compass reading of objects close to where the deer was standing when you shot.

When you get down, you can use the orange visual clues to guide you in the proper direction to look for your deer, and to make sure you're looking at the proper distance. Leaving a blaze orange hat or glove on the stand also tells hunting partners that you're looking for your deer.

Troy Przekurat
Wheeling, Illinois

While you're looking for your deer, leave some blaze orange back at your stand.

MAKE A THERMOS SOCK

Sitting on a deer stand takes patience, and patience requires comfort. Mornings are often cold, and I find that taking a thermos of coffee allows me to enjoy sitting on stand longer, thus improving my chances of seeing a deer. But a thermos is often cumbersome, and I prefer to keep my hands free while going to my stand.

Therefore, I've designed a "sock" that my thermos fits into, with a shoulder strap for carrying it. To make one, start with ½ yard of fleece. Measure the circumference of the thermos and cut the fleece ½ inch wider. Sew the edges together 2 inches longer than the thermos. Sew a ½-inch-wide piece of elastic at the bottom of the tube, and tie the ends of the elastic together, which will close the end in a circular pattern. Take the upper pieces of the fleece and sew them together to form a shoulder strap. The fleece will stretch to secure the thermos and to fit around your shoulder.

Chris Tennant
Pullman, Washington

CHRISTMAS TREESTAND

If you or someone you know is throwing out an old artificial Christmas tree, take some branches from it. The ones with bendable wire stems are great for adding a little cover to your treestand. Just wrap the metal ends with electrical tape or camo duct tape, and stick them through the base of your treestand platform. I also stick a couple through the chain links that hold my stand to the tree. This gives me cover all around. The branches can be bent to any position!

Bob Stayduhar
Braddock, Pennsylvania

KEY TO WARMTH: YOUR NECK

Look for old turtleneck shirts in earth-tone colors at garage sales and secondhand stores. They don't have to fit, because you will only need the collar area. Cut down through the top of each shoulder to mid-chest and back, effectively making a "dickie." This forms a "gasket" to prevent heat loss out your neck, and it also camouflages the area.

When the mercury climbs as the day wears on, or if you overheat, you can just pull the dickie off over your head without removing a layer of clothing. I always have several of these dickies in my duffel bag and pack. The system allows me to travel lighter and stay comfortable on stand while waiting for that cagey whitetail.

Jeff Bobrofsky
Lansing, Michigan

MARK THE RIGHT HEIGHT FOR HUNTING

When I locate a good tree for a stand in a new hunting area, I always climb the tree before the hunt. When I reach the height I can best see from, I tie a survey ribbon around the tree at nose height. I make the knot right at my nose. This way, when I climb before daylight in my climbing stand, I know when to stop climbing and the direction I should face (by making sure my nose is in front of the knot) to take advantage of adequate concealment and to provide the best field of view. Don't forget to remove the ribbon when you finish using the tree for the season.

Norman Ryan
Iowa, Louisiana

Tie a ribbon around your tree, right at nose height, so you know when to stop climbing next time.

ORGANIZE YOUR TREESTAND OR GROUND BLIND

Stowing and organizing your gear at your treestand or blind is always an issue. To solve the problem, make these versatile, inexpensive hooks.

Start by picking up a box of 3-inch galvanized Phillips-head deck screws and several feet of rubber vacuum line from an auto parts store. Cut the line into 1½-inch segments and thread a piece onto each screw. Put six into your pack, along with a stubby screwdriver. Screw several into the tree to accommodate your bow, calls and backpack.

The raw materials are simple and inexpensive (top), but the end results are quiet equipment hooks that do minimum harm to the tree (bottom).

The rubber keeps the hooks quiet, both in your pack and while in use, and protects your equipment too. These hooks can also be useful in ground blinds to keep gear off wet leaves or snow.

This system is less expensive than store-bought equipment hooks, and minimizes damage to the tree. They are easily removed at season's end or when you move your stand. If you are concerned about the scent of the rubber, leave the hooks outside a few days to air out before taking them to the woods.

*Jeff Bobrofsky
Lansing, Michigan*

PREVENT MUZZLELOADER MISFIRES

To prevent misfires with your muzzleloader: Before loading, run alcohol-soaked patches through the bore to remove any oil. If you own a flintlock, also wipe the pan and frizzen to ensure they're free of oil. Dry with clean patches. Use a squeeze bottle or dropper bottle to store the alcohol.

Michael M. Petronio
Pittsburgh, Pennsylvania

HANDY MUZZLELOADING NIPPLE PICK

Carry a safety pin attached to your jacket during muzzleloading season. After firing a couple of caps, I use the pin to push through the debris left in the nipple. After each shot, I use the pin again. I have never had a misfire since I began using a pin.

Daniel E. Burkowski
Oakland, Michigan

WATERPROOFING A MUZZLELOADER'S NIPPLE

On rainy or snowy days, I carry clear fingernail polish in my possibles bag. After putting on the percussion cap, I dab nail polish around the bottom edge of the cap. This keeps moisture out, so that the cap can do its job when called upon.

John Cripe
LaClede, Idaho

KEEP YOUR MUZZLELOADER DRY

If you use muzzleloaders, you know it is essential to avoid moisture and rust-preventative residue if you want more than the cap to go off. After 20-plus years of muzzleloading, I've developed a process to ensure my barrel is dry before I load the gun for hunting.

The process is simple and inexpensive. The only requirement is a supply of rubbing alcohol.

First, run several patches down the barrel, either dry or with solvent to remove your rust preventative. Then, while holding the finger of one hand over the nipple opening, use the other hand to pour a small amount of rubbing alcohol down the barrel. After a few seconds, let the alcohol run out onto a rag. Then run several patches soaked with rubbing alcohol up and down the barrel. Next, run several dry patches up and down the barrel.

Now set the barrel aside to allow any remaining alcohol to evaporate. Be sure all remaining alcohol has evaporated (this only takes a couple of minutes) before loading. Then follow your normal loading procedures, and keep your weapon dry during use. This procedure can also be used at the range to be sure the barrel is dry after cleaning with blackpowder solvent.

Alcohol removes all traces of oils, which can foul a load and cause it not to fire. Alcohol also displaces any moisture while leaving behind no residue.

Be sure to do this procedure in a well-ventilated area away from all flames.

Steven Shaffer
Cambridge, Ohio

MAKING A HEATED SCENT CANISTER

I have a homemade scent streamer that is easy to make. And best of all, it costs only cents to create. First, you need a soft-drink can and a filet knife. Cut the can in half at the UPC label, or about 2 inches from the bottom. Make a cut about 1½ inches long, down both sides of the can's top portion, starting at the open end of the can.

Insert the bottom of the can into the top portion. Cut a triangle into both sides of the can on the new bottom and bend them out flat. Poke a hole into each and insert a nail into each, which holds it down and keeps it from tipping over. Put a small tea candle into the bottom. Now put your favorite lure into the top and light the candle.

A = Bottom of can holds scent lure.
B = Top of can, upside down, houses candle.
C = Triangular cuts allow air in for flame.

A reworked soda can converts nicely into a brewing station for attracting bucks with warm, lively scent.

One note: Consider fire safety concerns; if the woods are tinder dry, you may want to wait for another day to use the scented heat canister.

Jeffrey L. Mensch
Dushore, Pennsylvania

SILENTLY STORE PERCUSSION CAPS

To keep extra percussion caps from rattling in their tin can, put two-sided tape inside the tin, and then stick 12 to 18 extra caps flat side to the tape. Use an old tin for this device.

John Cripe
LaClede, Idaho

CHALK IS CHEAP FOR TRACKING WIND

Some companies make a wind indicator that sprays an odorless powder into the air to check the wind direction. The devices sell for $2.50 to $3 for about 10 grams. Once the container is empty, you must buy another.

I have found that a great refill material is the chalk powder that building contractors use to mark straight lines with chalking reels. It's much cheaper, and it does the job just as well. You can buy 4-ounce refills in any do-it-yourself store and most discount stores for about $2.

This chalk is sold in many colors—such as orange, red, white and blue—and also as a bonus it can also be used to mark your way to your stand. Just spray a little on a tree as you walk by. It won't hurt the trees, and it takes a hard rain to wash it off.

Mike Koval
Cheyenne, Wyoming

Use an Old Suitcase to Treat Clothing

To control the scent of my hunting clothes, I use an old suitcase and line it with cedar branches. This gives my clothing a cedar smell. After a day's hunt, wash and dry your clothes, then put them in the suitcase to absorb the fresh cedar smell. If you hunt in other areas, use material from plants or trees that are prevalent in your area.

Dale Beisner
Natoma, Kansas

Store your hunting clothes with cedar branches, pine boughs or other vegetation native to your hunting area.

Wind Can Be Your Friend

Always use the wind to your advantage. I like to hunt when the wind is blowing hard. The deer are jumpier, but the wind muffles the sound of the steps you take and the mistakes you make. I can get closer to animals when the wind is blowing hard because they can't hear me as well. As long as you keep the wind in your face, this works extremely well.

Kody Jon Anderson
Fountain Green, Utah

Keep Your Towel Scent-Free

The next time you're washing your hunting clothes in descenting soap, throw in a bath towel with the load. You don't want to smell like one of those static-free dryer sheets, do you? Then on the day of your hunt, when you get out of the shower after using the descenting soap, you can dry off with a scent-free towel to beat the tremendously sensitive noses of trophy deer and elk.

Bruce Pistocco
Amarillo, Texas

TRIPLE-PURPOSE TREESTAND ROPE

Attach 50 feet of parachute cord to your climbing treestand. Then measure 3 feet from the stand and tie a knot. Continue tying knots every three feet until you reach the end. There will be 2 feet left. Attach a dog-collar clip to the end to secure your gun or bow (purpose one). The knots help you hold onto the rope when you pull up your gear (purpose two) and also help you estimate your height in the tree (purpose three).

Steven Ellison
Jacksonville, Arkansas

Knots in a rope are usually a pain, but in this case they're part of the plan.

SCENT-FREE CLOTHING TECHNIQUES

To help reduce odors in the deer woods, wash your hunting clothes in plain warm water. When the rinse cycle starts, add half a box of baking soda to the water and let the clothes rinse in it. Next, hang the clothes outside to dry, and then put them in an unscented trash bag with the remaining half box of baking soda inside the bag, and seal it overnight. This will reduce scent in and on your hunting clothes.

David Lowe
Huntsville, Tennessee

GROUND BLIND GOODIES

I've found ground blinds to be very effective, even though some people might say they are not. They are a lot safer than treestands. Your movement is well hidden. Your scent is held in by the walls of the blind. It is also easier to shoot from ground blinds because trees move in the wind; a ground blind doesn't. Plus, you don't have to deal with unknown shot angles when an animal is close.

Henry E. Bush
Sulligent, Alabama